異口同聲
vs.
Be of one voice

中英成語 800 對

陳永楨 陳善慈 張同 編著

商務印書館

本書例句部分由張同教授增補外，其餘內容乃節錄自本公司出版之《漢英對照成語詞典》。

異口同聲 vs. Be of one voice
——中英成語 800 對

編　　者：陳永楨　陳善慈

例句編寫：張　同（阿五）

責任編輯：鈕士敏

封面設計：張　毅

出　　版：商務印書館（香港）有限公司
香港筲箕灣耀興道 3 號東滙廣場 8 樓
http://www.commercialpress.com.hk

發　　行：香港聯合書刊物流有限公司
香港新界大埔汀麗路36號中華商務印刷大廈3字樓

印　　刷：美雅印刷製本有限公司
九龍官塘榮業街 6 號海濱工業大廈 4 樓 A

版　　次：2005 年 9 月第 1 版第 2 次印刷
© 商務印書館（香港）有限公司
ISBN 962 07 0263 8
Printed in Hong Kong

出版說明

人同此心，心同此理。有些想法，在中英成語裏都有相似的表達方式。出口成文，豈不更容易，更多樂趣？

本書選了800對中英都常用的成語，對比對照。成語條目主要選自陳永楨及陳善慈教授所編著，本館出版的《漢英對照成語詞典》；另特請張同（阿五）教授為800條詞目編寫例句，加強本書的內容。

每條對比的成語除了該成語的用法外，另提供同義詞及反義詞的說法；例句則教導讀者如何正確使用在日常用法中。成語故事二十則可讓讀者在學詞之餘，還能輕鬆地學習到成語的有趣故事及由來。

這是一本趣味和實用兼具的可閱讀可查閱的書，讓讀者在享受閱讀樂趣的同時，使中英語基礎都更上一層樓。

商務印書館編輯部

contents 目錄

中文成語	英文成語	

一 畫

二 畫

三　畫

四　畫

五　畫

六 畫

九　畫

十 畫

十一 畫

十三 畫

十四 畫

十五　畫

十六　畫

十七 畫

yí cùn guāng yīn yí cùn jīn

一寸光陰一寸金

Time is money.

There is nothing more precious than time.
Make the best of one's time.

例句 We have to work harder because **time is money**
which should not be wasted.

成語故事：Time is money

　　有人將此語譯作"一刻千金"，令人想起中國宋代詩
人蘇軾（蘇東坡，公元1063-1101）的詩句：春宵一刻值
千金。東坡先生詠的是春宵，當然不是此語所本。富蘭
克林（Benjamin Franklin，1706-1790）在 Poor Richard's
Almanack中列有此句作格言，有人以為是他的
創作，實際上此語在他之前已經存在。
因此有人考據認為它原是古老的俗諺，
經名人多次引用後成了流行的成語。

yī bù zuò èr bù xiū

一不做，二不休

What is worth doing at all is worth doing well.

In for a penny, in for a pound.
As well be hanged for a sheep as a lamb.
Over shoes, over boots.
Go the whole hog.

例句 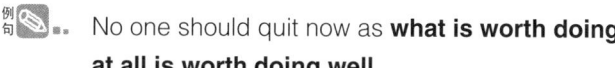 No one should quit now as **what is worth doing at all is worth doing well**.

出處 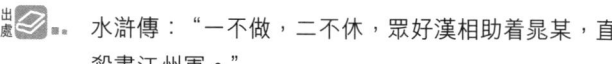 水滸傳："一不做，二不休，眾好漢相助着晁某，直殺盡江州軍。"

yí rì sān qiū

一日三秋

It seems ages.

Time hangs heavy on one's hand.
An eternity.

例句 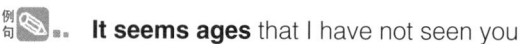 **It seems ages** that I have not seen you.

出處 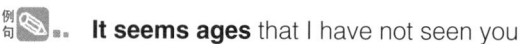 詩經・王風・采葛："彼采蕭兮，一日不見，如三秋兮。"

yì máo bù bá

一毛不拔

Not to part with the parings of one's nails.

As close as a clam.
As tight as a drum.
Be close-fisted.
Utterly stingy.

 He is a real miser who will **not part with the parings of his nails**.

 孟子‧盡心上：「揚子取為我，拔一毛而利天下，不為也。」

同義：吝嗇小氣　Cramp in the hand.
反義：仗義疏財　Come down handsome.

yí qù bú fù fǎn

一去不復返

Gone with the wind.

To be going for good and all.
Gone forever.
Have left for good.

例句 ■■ My purse has been stolen, **gone with the wind**.

出處 ■■ 崔顥．黃鶴樓詩：＂黃鶴一去不復返。＂

同義：杳如黃鶴　Nowhere to be found.

反義：捲土重來　Stage a comeback.

yì shī zú chéng qiān gǔ hèn
一失足成千古恨
One wrong step may bring a great fall.

One false move may lose the game.
Do wrong once and you'll never hear the end of it.

例句 ■■ Think twice before you take any action as **one wrong step may bring a great fall**.

yì běn zhèng jīng
一本正經
Look as if butter wouldn't melt in one's mouth.

Speak like a book.
Goody-goody.
Have a serious look.
Put on a solemn look.
Nice Nelly (Nellie).

✏️ James is very serious, with a **look as if butter wouldn't melt in his mouth**.

yì běn wàn lì
一本萬利
Light gains make heavy purses.

Make a scoop.
Reap a fat profit.

✏️ He bet on the right horse and **light gains made heavy purses**.

> **反義：**血本無歸　Sell one's hens on a rainy day.

yì fān fēng shùn
一帆風順
It's all plain sailing.

Sail before the wind.
It was roses all the way.
Without a hitch.
Godspeed! everything goes well.

✏️ They start to carry out their project and **it's all plain sailing**.

反義：命途多舛　The times are out of joint.

yì nián zhī jì zài yú chūn
一年之計在於春
April and May are the key of the year.

例句 ■■ It is important to make early decisions: a year's plan is in the spring.

出處 ■■ 南朝‧梁‧蕭繹‧纂要："一年之計在於春，一日之計在於晨。"

yì chéng bú biàn
一成不變
Hard and fast.

例句 ■■ The decision is made, **hard and fast**.

出處 ■■ 禮記‧王制："刑者型也，型者成也，一成而不可變。"

同義：原封不動　Keep intact.

反義：變幻莫測　The unexpected always happens.

一
畫

yí jiàn zhōng qíng
一見鍾情
Love at first sight.

Take an instant fancy to

例句  Lily married Ronald last week, a case of **love at first sight**.

yì yán jì chū sì mǎ nán zhuī
一言既出，駟馬難追
A word spoken is past recalling.

When the word is out, it belongs to another.

例句 We have to keep our promise, **a word spoken is past recalling**.

出處 宋・歐陽修・筆說："俗云，一言出口，駟馬難追。"

yí shì wú chéng
一事無成
Not a thing accomplished.

Have nothing to show for it.
All ended in smoke.

Lazy people lead a life **without a single accomplishment**.

 白居易·除夜寄微之詩："鬢毛不覺白毿毿，一事無成百不堪。"

> **反義：**從勝利走向勝利
> Nothing succeeds like success.

---

yí kè qiān jīn
一刻千金
Every minute counts.

Time is money.
Lost time is never found again.

 Hurry up to catch the bus, **every minute counts**!

 蘇軾·春夜詩："春宵一刻值千金。"

---

yì wǎng wú qián
一往無前
To go ahead with nothing in front.

Press forward.
Never to look back.
Carry all before one.

Never to look behind one.

 We shall **go ahead with nothing in front** to carry out our plan.

同義：勇往直前　Forge ahead.	

反義：開倒車　To back-pedal.	

yì bō wèi píng yì bō yòu qǐ
一波未平，一波又起
Wave after wave.

Hit one snag after another.
It never rains but it pours.
A run of bad luck.

 The work has been confronted with difficulties, **wave after wave**.

 姜夔‧白石道人詩說：「波瀾開闔，如在江湖中，一波未平，一波已作。」

同義：禍不單行　Misfortunes seldom come singly.	

反義：一帆風順　It's all plain sailing.	

yì zhī bàn jiě
一知半解
Have only a smattering of

Quarter flash and three parts foolish.
Holding the eel of science by the tail.
A little learning is a dangerous thing.
Tyro and smatterer.

例句  **Henry has only a smattering of** Latin.

出處 宋 · 嚴羽 · 滄浪詩話：" 有透徹之悟，有但得一知半解之悟。"

> **反義：**造詣甚深　To be at home in

yí miàn zhī jiāo
一面之交
A bowing acquainatance.

例句 I have **a bowing acquaintance** with Henry.

出處 袁宏 · 三國名臣序贊：" 徒以一面之交，定臧否之決。"

> **反義：**管鮑之誼　Damon and Pythias.

一
畫

yí qì hē chéng

一氣呵成

At a breath (stretch).

At one sitting.

例句 ■■ A good poem is usually accomplished with **one breath**.

出處 ■■ 清 · 李漁 · 閒情偶寄 · 賓白：「亦皆一氣呵成，無有斷續。」

同義：貫徹始終 Such beginning, such end.
反義：或作或輟 Off and on.

yì zhēn jiàn xiě

一針見血

Put one's finger on

String to the quick.
Hit the right nail on the head.
Touch one on the raw.

例句 ■■ Your comment **puts your finger on** his speech.

yì mǎ dāng xiān

一馬當先

To be in the van (lead).

Break a path.
Show the way.

 In the football match, Johon is alway **in the van**.

同義：遙遙領先　Streets ahead of	
反義：畏縮不前　Back out of	

yí bài tú dì

一敗塗地

Down to the ground.

Lick the dust.
To land with a thud.
Down and out.
Knocked into a cocked hat.
Get the worst of it.
To be left at the post.
To come off crabs.

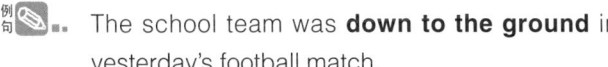

例句 ■■ The school team was **down to the ground** in yesterday's football match.

出處 ■■ 史記 · 高祖本紀："天下方擾，諸侯並起，今置將不善，一敗塗地。"

同義：潰不成軍　To be put to rout.

反義：所向披靡　To carry all before one.

yì pín rú xǐ
一貧如洗

As poor as a church mouse.

Be down and out.

Be hard up.

On one's uppers.

One's hair grows through one's hood.

例句 ■■ With his company went bankrupt, Robert is now **as poor as a church mouse**.

同義：不名一文　Have not a penny to bless oneself with.

反義：腰纏萬貫　Roll in wealth.

yì bǐ gōu xiāo
一筆勾銷
All annulled.

Cancel out.
Write off at a stroke.
Get even with

 The treaty is **all annulled**.

 宋史："范十二丈一筆勾去，焉知一家哭矣。"

yí shì tóng rén
一視同仁
When it rains it rains on all alike.

The sun shines upon all alike.
The sea has fish for every man.
Not to make chalk of one and cheese of another.
Without discrimination.

 Don't expect favours from the boss as he thinks
that **when it rains it rains on all alike**.

 韓愈·原人："一視而同仁。"

同義：等量齊觀　　Put on a par.
反義：區別對待　　Make fish of one and flesh of another.

一
畫

yì tā hú tú

一塌糊塗

A pretty kettle of fish.

A devil of a mess.

 The solution is so poor that it turned the situation into **a pretty kettle of fish**.

同義：亂七八糟　At sixes and sevens.
反義：有條不紊　In apple-pie order.

yí yì gū xíng

一意孤行

Take the law into one's hand.

Go one's own way.
Take the bit in one's mouth (teeth).

 He **took the law into his (own) hand** and sold the house.

 史記‧張湯列傳："絕知友賓客之請，孤立行一意而已。"

同義：一言堂　Lay down the law.
反義：集思廣益　Lay our heads together.

yí luò qiān zhàng

一落千丈

To go to pot.

To touch bottom.
A total failure.

 Business has **gone to pot** and they have to close down the shop.

 韓愈‧聽穎師彈琴詩："躋攀分寸不可上，失勢一落千丈強。"

同義：江河日下　Go down drain.
反義：飛黃騰達　His star was in the ascendant.

yì míng jīng rén

一鳴驚人

Come as a bombshell.

Make a noise in the world.
To startle the world.

 Joan's debut **came as a bombshell** in Broadway, applauded by the press.

出處 ■■ 史記・滑稽列傳："此鳥不飛則已，一飛沖天，不鳴
則已，一鳴驚人。"

反義：默默無聞　To be a nobody.

yí jiàn shuāng diāo
一箭雙鵰
Kill two birds with one stone (shaft).

例句 ■■ Robert wishes to marry a rich girl; to **kill two birds
with one stone**, he said.

出處 ■■ 唐書："高駢見二鵰並飛，駢曰，我且貴，當中之。
一發貫二鵰焉。"

同義：一舉兩得　To cut both ways.

yí fà qiān jūn
一髮千鈞
Hang by a thread.

At moment of danger.

例句 ■■ He was so badly hurt in the accident that the doc-
tors said his life was **hanging by a thread**.

出處 ■■ 韓愈 · 與孟尚書書： "其危如一髮引千鈞。"

> **同義：**危在旦夕　Hang on by the eyelids.

yí nuò qiān jīn
一諾千金

A promise worth thousand gold.

Words as good as gold.
The promise of a man of faith.
To be as good as one's word.

 例句 ■■ A gentleman's agreement is **a promise worth thousand gold**.

 出處 ■■ 史記 · 季布欒布列傳： "得黃金百斤，不如得季布一諾。"

> **反義：**人而無信，不知其可也
> 　　　　He that has lost his credit is dead to the world.

yì jǔ chéng míng
一舉成名

Make a name for oneself.

Make a mark in the world.

一畫

To rise to fame.
To come into one's own
Rocket to fame.
Become famous overnight.

例句 .. A scholar in the past studied hard for years to **make a name for himself**.

出處 .. 韓愈·竇公墓誌銘：〝公一舉成名而東。〞

> **反義**：身敗名裂　Fall into disgrace.

yì jǔ liǎng dé
一舉兩得

Kill two flies with one slap.

Stop two gaps with one bush.
Catch two pigeons with on bean.
To cut both ways.

例句 .. The police arrested the thief and his brother to **kill two flies with one slap**.

出處 .. 東觀漢記·耿弇傳：〝所謂一舉而兩得者也。〞

> **反義**：兩頭落空　Fall between two stools.

yí qiào bù tōng

一竅不通

All Greek to one.

A babe in the woods.
A total greenhorn.

 Shanghai dialect is **all Greek to people** in Canton.

 呂氏春秋注："紂心不通，安於為惡，若其一竅通，則比干不殺矣。"

> **反義**：滿腹經綸　To give chapter and verse.

yí pù shí hán

一曝十寒

By fits and snatches (starts).

 Nothing can be done by doing it **by fits and snatches**.

 孟子·告子上："雖有天下易生之物也，一日暴之，十日寒之，未有能生者也。"

> **反義**：堅持不懈　Peg away at it.

一

畫

yí cù ér jiù

一蹴而就

At one stroke.

Succeed overnight.

Take something all in one stride.

To start with a bang.

例句 ■. Do not expect to finish the job **at one stroke**.

出處 ■. 宋 · 蘇洵 · 上田樞密書：「天下之學者，孰不欲一蹴而造聖人之域。」

同義：旗開得勝　Get off to a flying start.
反義：功敗垂成　A slip betwixt the cup and the lip.

yì chóu mò zhǎn

一籌莫展

To be at one's wit's end.

例句 ■. I am **at my wit's end** when you ask me to solve the problem for you.

出處 ■. 宋史 · 蔡幼學傳：「多士盈庭而一籌不吐。」

同義：黔驢技窮	At the end of one's tether.
反義：心生一計	Hit upon an idea.

jiǔ niú èr hǔ zhī lì

九牛二虎之力

Strain every nerve.

Move heaven and earth to

 The rescue team **strained every nerve** to get the boy out from the fire.

同義：全力以赴	To go all out.
反義：不費吹灰之力	A lift of the finger.

rén shān rén hǎi

人山人海

A sea of faces.

 You can see **a sea of faces** at the airport to welcome the astronaut.

rén bù kě yǐ mào xiàng

人不可以貌相

Beauty is but skin-deep.

Never judge from appearances.
It is not the hood that makes the monk.

 All flowers will fade, **beauty is but skin-deep**.

> 反義：先敬羅衣後敬人
>
>   Good clothes open all doors.

rén yún yì yún

人云亦云

Echo one's every word.

Pin one's faith upon another's sleeve.
Repeat like a parrot.
To say ditto.

 Robert is an **echo of** his wife's opinions.

蔡松年．槽聲同彥高賦詩："他日人云我亦云。"

> 同義：隨聲附和　To chime in.

> 反義：別開生面　Break fresh ground.

rén yán kě wèi
人言可畏
Opinion rules the world.

If all men say that thou art an ass, then bray.
What will Mr. Grundy say?
Fling dirt enough and some will stick.
We are all slaves of opinion.

例句 Watch your deeds as **opinion rules the world**.

出處 詩經 · 鄭風 · 將仲子： "人之多言，亦可畏也。"

> **反義**：笑罵由他笑罵，好官我自為之
> Hard words break no bones.

rén dìng shèng tiān
人定勝天
Everyone is the maker of his own fate.

例句 Do your best and remind yourself that **everyone is the maker of his own fate**.

出處 劉祁 · 歸潛志： "天定能勝人，人定亦能勝天。"

> **反義**：人算不如天算
> An ounce of luck is better than a pound of wisdom.

二
畫

rén fēi shèng xián shú néng wú guò

人非聖賢，孰能無過

No one is without his faults.

例句 ▪▪ Do not blame yourself for the mistake, **no one is without his faults**.

出處 ▪▪ 左傳·宣二年："人誰無過。"

> **同義**：人誰無過　He is lifeless that is faultless.

rén fú yú shì

人浮於事

Too many cooks spoil the broth.

To be over-staffed.

例句 ▪▪ It only takes two to do the job, **too many cooks spoil the broth**.

出處 ▪▪ 禮記·坊記："君子與其使食浮於人也，寧使人浮於食。"

> **同義**：三個和尚沒水吃
> Everybody's business is nobody's business.

> **反義**：精兵簡政
> I will keep no more cats than will catch mice.

rù mù sān fēn

入木三分

Give a vivid picture of

Cut to the quick.
Leave an indelible impression on

 His description **gives a vivid picture of** the situation.

張懷瓘 · 書斷："晉王羲之書祝版，工人削之，筆入木三分。"

同義：印象深刻　Borne in upon one.
反義：輕描淡寫　Touch on lightly.

rù xiāng suí sú

入鄉隨俗

Do in Rome as the Romans do.

To go native.

 I take tea instead of coffee when I visit my native town, **do in Rome as the Romans do**.

二畫

lì bù cóng xīn

力不從心

The spirit is willing, but the flesh is weak.

Beyond one's tether.

 Robert worked very hard but failed in the examination, **the spirit is willing but the flesh is weak**.

 漢書 · 班超傳：「如有卒暴，超之氣力不能從心。」

> **同義**：心有餘而力不足
> Bite off more than one can chew.

lì bù shēng rèn

力不勝任

Beyond one.

Beyond one's power.
To be far below the mark.
Not cut out for

 He is **beyond one**, not able to do the job.

 易 · 繫辭：「鼎折足，覆公餗，其形渥，凶，言不勝其任也。」

> **反義**：勝任愉快　Equal to the occasion.

shí nián shù mù   bǎi nián shù rén

十年樹木，百年樹人

A skill is not acquired in a matter of days.

Rome was not built in a day.

例句 ▪▪ It takes the worker five years to learn his trade, **a skill is not acquired in a matter of days**.

出處 ▪▪ 管子・權修："十年之計，莫如樹木。終身之計，莫如樹人。"

shí ná jiǔ wěn

十拿九穩

Ten to one.

Feel cork (pretty) sure.
To have taken for granted.
Have in the bag.
Safe bind, safe find.
With hands down.

例句 ▪▪ I bet you **ten to one** that Robert will win the game.

出處 ▪▪ 阮大鋮・燕子箋："此是十拿九穩，必中的計策。"

shí wàn huǒ jí

十萬火急

In hot haste.

S. O. S.

Not a moment to lose.

 John needed the money **in hot haste**, send it to him immediately.

同義：火燒眉毛	Imminent danger.
反義：慢條斯理	At a snail's pace.

sān shí liù jì zǒu wéi shàng jì

三十六計，走為上計

Keep out of the way.

Take flight.

Give one the slip.

Give leg-bail.

Take to one's legs.

 Keep out of the way to avoid any risk.

 齊書・王敬則傳："檀公（檀道濟）三十六策，走為上計。"

> **同義**：溜之大吉　Seek safety in flight.

sān sī ér hòu xíng
三思而後行
Look before you leap.

Measure thrice before you cut once.
He thinks not well that thinks not again.
Second thoughts are best.
To sleep on a matter.

 If you want to do it right, **look before you leap**.

 論語‧公冶長："季文子三思而後行，子聞之曰，再斯可矣。"

> **同義**：深思熟慮　Turn it over in one's mind.

> **反義**：冒失從事　Buy a pig in a poke.

sān jiān qí kǒu
三緘其口
Button up one's lip.

One's lips are sealed.

Hold one's peace.

To hush up.

To clam up.

例句 ▪▪ If you do not know the truth, you better **button up your lip**.

出處 ▪▪ 家語："孔子觀周，入后稷之廟，有金人焉，三緘其口而銘其背曰，古之慎言人也。"

同義：守口如瓶　As close as an oyster.
反義：喋喋不休　Talk the hind leg off a donkey.

shàng xíng xià xiào

上行下效

Where the dam leaps over, the kid follows.

As the old cock crows, the young one learns.

例句 ▪▪ "The director of a department must be prompt to arrive in the morning, **where the dam leaps over, the kid follows**.

出處 ▪▪ 意林・引崔寔・政論："上行下效，然謂之教。"

jiǔ hàn féng gān yǔ
久旱逢甘雨
Feeling a sense of relief.

A sight for sore eyes.

例句 ✎ ▪▪ John's timely loan gives poor Robert **a sense of feeling relief**.

出處 ✑ ▪▪ 容齋隨筆："久旱逢甘雨，他鄉遇故知，洞房花燭夜，金榜掛名時。"

> **反義**：屋漏更兼連夜雨　It never rains but it pours.

wáng yáng bǔ láo wèi wéi wǎn yě
亡羊補牢，未為晚也
It is better late than never.

It is never too late to mend.

例句 ✎ ▪▪ I must give my answer to John today; **it is better late than never**.

出處 ✑ ▪▪ 戰國策 · 楚策四："亡羊補牢，未為晚也。"

> **反義**：悔之晚矣　Repentance comes too late.

qiān fāng bǎi jì

千方百計

By hook and by crook.

Explore every avenue.
Resort to every trick.
Leave no stone unturned.
In all manner of ways.
Try one's utmost.
Do everthing possible.

例句 ▪▪ Robert tried **by hook and by crook** to get the treasure but failed.

出處 ▪▪ 朱子語錄：“譬如捉賊相似，須是著起精神，千方百計去趕捉他。”

qiān lǐ sòng é máo wù qīng qíng yì zhòng

千里送鵝毛，物輕情意重

A token of affection.

What is bought is cheaper than a gift.

例句 ▪▪ Please accept my gift as **a token of affection**.

出處 ▪▪ 邢俊臣詞：“物輕人意重，千里送鵝毛。”

qiān jūn yí fà

千鈞一髮

At the critical moment.

To hang by a thread.

例句 ■■ He gave his right hand to me **at the critical moment**.

出處 ■■ 韓愈·與孟尚書書："其危如一髮引千鈞。"

qiān zǎi nán féng

千載難逢

It only happens once in a blue moon.

It chances in an hour that happens not in seven years.

例句 ■■ For a miser like Robert to invite you for dinner, **it only happens once in a blue moon**.

> 反義：司空見慣　Order of the day.

qiān chuí bǎi liàn

千錘百煉

Steeled and tempered.

A good anvil does not fear the hammer.

Through the mill.
Gone through fire and water.

 Steeled and tempered in the dog-eats-dog world, John is able to overcome all difficulties.

 趙翼‧甌北詩話：〝詩家好作奇句警語，必千錘百煉而後能成。〞

kǒu shì xīn fēi
口是心非

Act the part of a do-gooder.

Speak with one's tongue in one's cheek.
Say one thing and mean another.
Play a double game.

 Nobody trusts that guy who always **acts the part of a do-gooder**.

 葛洪‧抱朴子‧微旨：〝若乃憎善好殺，口是心非，背向異辭，反戾直正……凡有一事，輒是一罪。〞

同義：言不由衷　To be mealy-mouthed.
反義：心口如一 What the heart thinks the tongue speaks.

kǒu ruò xuán hé

口若懸河

Rattle on

Talk nine words at once.

 The speaker **rattles on**, but nobody pays any attention to his speech.

 劉義慶‧世說新語‧賞譽："郭子玄語議如懸河瀉水，注而不竭。"

同義：滔滔不絕　Talk oneself out of breath.
反義：期期艾艾　Hem and haw.

kǒu mì fù jiàn

口蜜腹劍

A honey tongue, a heart of gall.

Bees that have honey in their mouths have stings in their tails.
To be nasty-nice.

 Beware of those people who have **a honey tongue but a heart of gall**.

 資治通鑑‧唐紀："世謂李林甫口有蜜，腹有劍。"

同義：笑裏藏刀　Velvet paws hide sharp claws.

shì bié sān rì　guā mù xiāng kàn

士別三日，刮目相看

Naughty boys sometimes make good men.

Wanton kittens may make sober cats.
An ugly duckling.

例句 John graduated with high honor from senior high school, **naughty boys sometimes make good men**.

出處 三國志 · 呂蒙傳注："士別三日，即當刮目相待。"

同義：非復吳下阿蒙　The ugly duckling.

dà gōng wú sī

大公無私

Fair field and no favour.

The balance distinguishes not between gold and lead.

例句 A good boss should deal with all workers in **fair field and no favour**.

龔自珍‧龔定庵集‧論私："且今之大公無私者，有楊墨之賢耶。"

同義：捨己為人　To bell the cat.

反義：假公濟私　To practise jobbery.

dà gōng gào chéng
大功告成
Come off with honours.

Bring home the bacon.
Come through with flying colours.

 Our efforts **come off with honours** at last.

反義：功虧一簣
Another course would have done it.

dà dǎ chū shǒu
大打出手
Come to blows.

Fall together by the ears.
Come to grips with

例
句 ✏ ▪ ▪ They argued first and then **came to blows**.

同義：拳腳交加　Cuffs and kicks.
反義：相安無事　Get along fairly well.

dà tóng xiǎo yì
大同小異
Much of a muchness.

There's not a pin to choose between them.

例
句 ✏ ▪ ▪ John and Robert dressed **much of a muchness**.

出
處 📙 ▪ ▪ 唐・盧同・玉川子詩集・與馬異結交："同不同，異
自異，是謂大同而小異。"

同義：不相上下 　　　As well be hanged for a sheep as for a lamb.
反義：判若雲泥　A world of difference.

dà chuī dà léi
大吹大擂
Brag about

Bluff and bluster.

A flourish of trumpets.
Make much of

例句 ■• He always **brags about** his past record.

出處 ■• 元曲選 · 賈仲名 · 蕭淑蘭： "小的每與我大吹大擂者。"

同義：大張旗鼓　With great fanfare.

反義：偃旗息鼓　Draw in one's horns.

---

dà xiāng jìng tíng

大相徑庭

Poles apart

The opposite.
At odds with
At loggerheads.

例句 ■• There is not a thing they have in common-in thought and ideas they are **poles apart**.

出處 ■• 莊子 · 逍遙遊： "大有徑庭，不近人情。"

反義：同心協力　Unite as one.

---

dà huò bù jiě

大惑不解

Beyond comprehension.

Beyond one.
Can make neither head nor tail of

例句 The government's policy is **beyond comprehension** of most of us.

出處 莊子‧天地：“大惑者終身不解，大愚者終身不靈。”

同義：莫名其妙　To be at sea.
反義：心中有數　Know what's what.

dà zhì ruò yú

大智若愚

Still waters run deep.

No man can play the fool so well as the wise man.
He is not a wise man who cannot play the fool on occasion.

例句 Silent man, like **still waters, runs deep** and dangerous.

出處 老子：“大智若愚。”

同義：深藏若虛	To humble oneself.
反義：不懂裝懂	Assume a knowing air.

dà fā léi tíng
大發雷霆

Come down like a ton of bricks.

Explode with rage.

Fly into one's tantrums.

 The boss **came down like a ton of bricks** when he learned the bad news.

 三國志·吳志·陸遜傳："今不忍小忿而發雷霆之怒。"

同義：暴跳如雷	Stamp with fury.
反義：忍氣吞聲	Swallow the leek.

dà kāi yǎn jiè
大開眼界

Open a person's eyes.

Broaden one's horizon.

See the elephant.

An eye-opener.

 Travelling **opens a person's eyes** to the outside world.

> **反義**：目光如豆　See no further than one's nose.

dà shì yǐ qù
大勢已去
The day (field) is lost.

Come out of the little end of the horn.
Thursday come, and the week is gone.

 The captain saw that the ship began to sink and knew that **the day is lost**.

> **反義**：形勢大好　The goose hang high.

dà shā fēng jǐng
大殺風景
A wet blanket.

A fly in the ointment.
Take all the fun out of

His cruel remarks puts **a wet blanket** on the party.

李義山·雜纂："其一日殺風景。謂清泉濯足，花上曬褌，背山起樓，燒琴煮鶴，對花啜茶，松下喝道也。"

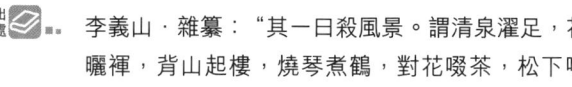

成語故事：Rome was not built in a day

　　古羅馬傳說中的羅馬建國者羅莫洛斯（Romulus）和萊莫斯（Remus）在第伯爾河（Tiber）畔建立的"永恆之城"（Eternal City），成為羅馬帝國拓展的中心。由一個小城市國家的中心發展成大帝國的城市，不是旦夕可成的。由於羅馬的宏偉建設是經過多年建造而成，因此以此諺喻大事業的建立非旦夕之功。西班牙作家塞萬第斯（Cervantes，1547-1616）在名著"唐吉訶德"（Don Quixte，亦作"瘋俠傳"）中曾引用此語。

dà qì wǎn chéng

大器晚成

Rome was not built in a day.

The best fruits are slowest in ripening.

 Don't push the boy too hard, **Rome was not built in a day**.

老子：〝大方無隅，大器晚成。〞

> **同義：**十年樹木，百年樹人
> A skill is not acquired in a matter of days.

dà xiǎn shēn shǒu

大顯身手

Have the field to oneself.

To try one's hand.
Show one's metal (mettle).
Have the field before one.

 James played the game and **had the field to oneself**.

> **反義：**冷眼旁觀　To be outside the ropes.

dà jīng xiǎo guài
大驚小怪
Much matter of a wooden platter.

Like a hen with one chicken.
A storm in a teacup.
Go off the deep end.
Much ado about nothing.
Look like a dying duck in a thunderstorm.
Make a song and dance about something.

 Such things happened very often, don't be **much matter of a wooden platter**.

> **反義：**若無其事　As if nothing has happened.

cùn bù bù lí
寸步不離
At one's elbow (heels).

Hover over

 They love each other very much, the wife is always **at her husband's elbow**.

> **同義：**緊跟　Follow hard after.

> **反義：**避之則吉　Steer clear of

cùn cǎo bù liú

寸草不留

To lay waste.

Stripped bare.

 The land had been **laid waste** before they built the factory.

同義：劃草除根　Pluck up by the roots.

xiǎo xīn yì yì

小心翼翼

Very gingerly.

Pay minute attention.
Mind one's P's and Q's.

 We present our case to the boss **very gingerly**.

詩經‧大雅‧文王："維此文王，小心翼翼。"

反義：莽莽撞撞　Like a bull in a china shop.

xiǎo wū jiàn dà wū
小巫見大巫

Not measure up to

The moon is not seen where the sun shines.
To be cast into the shade.

 He can **not measure up to** that man's ability.

 莊子 · 逸篇："小巫見大巫，拔茅而棄，此其所以終身弗如。"

> **同義：**相形見絀　Cast into the shade.

xiǎo tí dà zuò
小題大做

Make a mountain out of a molehill.

A tempest in a teapot.
A storm in a teacup.
Break a butterfly on a wheel.
Fuss about trifles.
Great cry and little wool.

 To treat him so well is to **make a mountain out of a molehill**.

> **同義：**張大其詞　Draw the long bow.

> **反義：**大題小做
> The mountain has brought forth a mouse.

shān yǔ yù lái fēng mǎn lóu
山雨欲來風滿樓
A storm is brewing.

When the clouds are upon the hills, they'll come down
　　by the mills.

 A glance through the editorials, we sense that **a**
　　(political) **storm is brewing**.

 許渾·咸陽城東樓詩："溪雲初起日沈閣，山雨欲來
　　風滿樓。"

shān qióng shuǐ jìn
山窮水盡
At the end of one's rope.

To be on the rocks.
At low water-mark.
Down to one's bottom dollar.

三
畫

He has lost his saving and finds himself **at the end of his rope**.

---

jǐ suǒ bú yù　wù shī yú rén
己所不欲，勿施於人
Do as you would be done by

Do not do unto others as you do not like them to do to you.

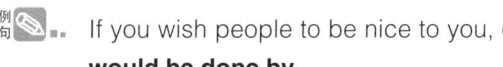 If you wish people to be nice to you, **do as you would be done by**.

論語 · 顏淵："其恕乎，己所不欲，勿施於人。"

---

bù rù hǔ xué yān dé hǔ zǐ
不入虎穴，焉得虎子
Nothing venture, nothing have (gain).

No pains, no gain.

Go and ask your boss to give you a promotion. **Nothing venture, nothing have**.

後漢書 · 班超傳："班超使西域，謂其官屬曰，不入虎穴，不得虎子。"

bù kě yí shì
不可一世
As proud (vain) as a peacock.

Puffed up with pride.
As proud as Lucifer.

 When John learned that he has got the scholarship, he was **as proud as a peacock**.

同義：昂首雲外　Have one's nose in the air.
反義：無面目見江東父老 　　　To fly from the face of men.

bù kě tóng rì ér yǔ
不可同日而語
Can't be mentioned on the same day.

Not to be mentioned in the same breath.
Not to be lumped together.

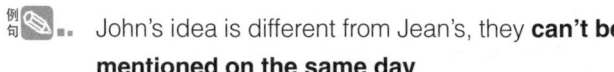 John's idea is different from Jean's, they **can't be mentioned on the same day**.

漢書・息夫躬傳：“臣與祿（公孫祿）異議，未可同日語也。”

> **反義：**相提並論　Place on par.

bù kě jiù yào
不可救藥
Beyond remedy.

If physic do not work, prepare for the kirk.

 Robert's laziness is **beyond remedy**.

 詩經・大雅："多將熇熇，不可救藥。"

> **同義：**病入膏肓　Too far gone.

> **反義：**微感不適　To feel off colour.

bù tóng fán xiǎng
不同凡響
Out of the common run.

Out of the ordinary.

 His performance on the stage is **out of the common run**.

> **同義**：技藝超倫
> Able to kick the eye out of a mosquito.

bù míng yì wén
不名一文

Have not a penny to bless oneself with

Have no face but one's own.
Not a feather to fly with
To be on the hocks.

例句 ▪ Donald is broken, **having not a penny to bless himself with**.

出處 ▪ 漢書・鄧通傳：「竟不得名一錢，寄死人家。」

> **同義**：阮囊羞澀　Not to have a bean.

> **反義**：腰纏萬貫　Roll in wealth.

bú zì liàng lì
不自量力

Go beyond one's depth.

Overreach oneself.
Bite off more than one can chew.

Throw straws against the wind.

 Trying to solve that problem is to **go beyond her depth** for Lily.

 戰國策・齊策三："荊甚固，而薛亦不量其力。"

同義：螳臂擋車　Kick against the pricks.

反義：人貴有自知之明　Know myself.

bù yán ér yù
不言而喻
It goes without saying.

Needless to say.

 It goes without saying that the truth is on our side.

同義：不在話下　To be taken for granted.

bù qū bù náo
不屈不撓
Stick to one's colours.

Firm and unyielding.

Fight for it tooth and nail.

Hang on by the eyelashes.

Keep one's chin up

As steady as a rock.

例句 ■■ To gain confidence of others for your idea, you have to **stick to your colours**.

出處 ■■ 漢書・敘傳下：「樂昌篤實，不撓不屈。」

同義：百折不撓　Stick it out.

反義：俯首就範　Give one's head for the washing.

bù zhī suǒ cuò

不知所措

At a loss what to do.

Stand at gaze.

To be at loose ends.

To be up a tree.

例句 ■■ He was **at a loss as to what he should do** next.

出處 ■■ 三國志・吳志・諸葛恪傳：「哀喜交並，不知所措。」

同義：六神無主　To be all at sea.

反義：胸有成竹　Have an ace up one's sleeve.

bù xiāng shàng xià

不相上下

On a par with

Much of a muchness.
Break even.
As well be hanged for a sheep as for a lamb.
A dead heat.
On a dead level with

 The way John seeks to solve the question is **on a par with** mine.

同義：半斤八兩
Six of one and half a dozen of the other.
反義：相去十萬八千里　Poles apart.

bù lún bú lèi

不倫不類

Neither fish, flesh, nor fowl, nor good red herring.

Neither rhyme nor season.

 No one likes her new chess; it is **neither fish, flesh, nor fowl, nor good red herring**.

 禮記：〝儗人不於其倫。〞／晉書：〝抗明威以儳不類。〞

同義：非驢非馬　Neither hawk nor buzzard.

bù róng zhì yí
不容置疑
Beyond all questions.

It leaves no room for doubt.

 It is **beyond all questions** that you will get the scholarship.

同義：毫無疑義　A moral certainty.

反義：難以置信　To stagger belief.

bú xiè yí gù
不屑一顧
Shut one's eyes to

Snap one's fingers at
Turn up one's nose at
To set at naught.
Fly in the face (teeth) of

 You can not **shut your eyes to** the reality.

同義：漠然置之 Look on with unconcern.
反義：不可輕視 Not to be taken lightly.

bù chǐ xià wèn

不恥下問

Bow down thy ear.

Though old and wise, yet still advise.
It is lawful to learn even from an enemy.

例句 ■■ The teacher **bowed down the ear** to one of his students, asking him what one should do in such situation.

出處 ■■ 論語："敏而好學，不恥下問。"

反義：剛愎自用 Reckon without one's host.

bù piān bù yǐ

不偏不倚

Hold the scale even.

Sit on the rail.
Betwixt and between.

When making a judgement, one has to **hold the scale even**.

> **同義**：一視同仁
> Not to make chalk of one and cheese of another.

> **反義**：厚此薄彼
> Make chalk of one and cheese of the other.

bú dòng shēng sè

不動聲色

Set one's face like a flint.

Keep a straight face.
Keep one's countenance.
Bit one's lips.
Keep quiet.
As quiet as a mouse.

 He sat there, **setting his face like a flint**, and tried to find out who was the suspect.

> **同義**：面不改容　Without turning a hair.

> **反義**：虛張聲勢　Barking dogs seldom bite.

bú sù zhī kè

不速之客

An unbidden guest.

A gate-crasher.

Turn up like a bad shilling.

He that comes uncalled sits unserved.

He that comes unbidden goes unthanked.

例句 ■■ Joseph came to the party as **an unbidden guest**.

出處 ■■ 周易・需：「有不速之客三人來。」

bù hán ér lì

不寒而慄

Make one's teeth chatter.

Make one's flesh creep.

例句 ■■ The mysterious sound in the dark **made Lily's teeth chattered**.

出處 ■■ 史記・酷吏列傳：「是日皆報殺四百餘人，其後郡中不寒而慄。」

四
畫

bù qī ér yù
不期而遇
To happen upon

To meet up with
To chance upon
To come across
Bump into someone.
Fall in with

 The two men **happened upon** each other by chance.

 穀梁傳・隱八年：〝不期而會曰遇。〞

> **同義：**邂逅相遇　Run into someone.

bú fèi chuī huī zhī lì
不費吹灰之力
A lift of the finger.

There's nothing to it.
Can do it on one's head.
As easy as pie.

 For John, **a lift of the finger** will do to finish the job.

> **同義：**易如反掌　As easy as winking.

> **反義：**九牛二虎之力　Move heaven and earth to

bù guǎn sān qī èr shí yī
不管三七二十一
Rain or shine.

Let the world wag as it will.
Come what may.
For good or ill.

 We have to carry out the plan, **rain or shine**.

> **反義：**瞻前顧後　Take a look around.

bù yí yú lì
不遺餘力
For all one is worth.

Leave no avenue unexplored.
Leave no stone unturned.
Go to all lengths.
Tooth and nail.
Move heaven and earth.

He will support you **for all he is worth**.

 戰國策："王曰，秦之攻我也，不遺餘力矣，必以倦而歸也。"

同義：開足馬力　At full steam.	

反義：袖手旁觀　Stand by with folded arms.	

bú yì ér fēi

不翼而飛

Vanish from sight.

Nowhere to be found.

 Don't leave your purse there, it will **vanish from sight** in no time.

 列子："珠無脛而行，玉無翼而飛。"

bù shí tái jǔ

不識抬舉

Bring a cow to the hall and she will run to the byre.

Give him enough rope and he will hang himself.

四
畫

To recommand Jack for the job is to **bring a cow to the hall (and she will run to the byre)**.

> **同義**：不堪造就
>
> Of a pig's tail you can never make a good shaft.

zhōng yōng zhī dào
中庸之道
The golden mean.

Steer a middle course.
Safety lies in the middle course.
Moderation in all things.

 The safe way is to follow **the golden mean**.

> **同義**：允執厥中　Follow the golden mean.

> **反義**：無所不用其極　Stick at nothing.

zhōng bǎo sī náng
中飽私囊
Line one's pocket.

Feather one's nest.

The corrupted official took the money to **line his pocket**.

同義：貪污腐化	Have an itching palm.
反義：廉潔清正	With clean hands.

jǐng jǐng yǒu tiáo
井井有條
In apple-pie order.

Keep everything ship-shape.

 The room maid has put the room **in apple-pie order**.

出處 荀子‧儒效："井井兮其有條理也。"

反義：雜亂無章	All in a muddle (mess).

四畫

wǔ shí bù xiào bǎi bù
五十步笑百步
An inch in a miss is as good as an ell.

A miss is as good as a mile.
A failure by however little is still a failure.

The pot calls the kettle black.

One ass nicknames another "Long ears".

例句  The pot calls the kettle black is **an inch in a miss as good as an ell**.

出處 🔖 ▪ 孟子 · 梁惠王上：" 棄甲曳兵而走，或百步而後止，或五十步而後止。以五十步笑百步，則何如。"

wǔ tǐ tóu dì

五體投地

Take one's hat to

On all fours.

Throw oneself at of someone's feet.

Hold a person in high esteem.

Fall on one's knees.

例句 ✏ ▪ I **take my hat** (off) **to** you, you did a good job.

出處 🔖 ▪ 楞嚴經：" 五體投地，長跪合掌，而白佛言。"

同義：甘拜下風　Sit at a person's feet.
反義：鼻子朝天　Cock up the nose.

rén zhě jiàn rén zhì zhě jiàn zhì

仁者見仁，智者見智

A matter of opinion.

Views vary from person to person.
Everything is as you take it.
Every man to his own taste.
Tastes differ.
Different things appeal to different people.

 Whether the plan will work or not is **a matter of opinion**.

 周易・繫辭上："仁者見之謂之仁，知者見之謂之知。"

四
畫

liù shén wú zhǔ

六神無主

To go to pieces.

To be all at sea.

 Since his wife's death, Jones has **gone (all) to pieces**.

 類函："黃帝問玄女兵法，此為六神，為戰主也。"

同義：魂飛魄散　Like a hog in a squall.	
反義：心中有數　Know one's own mind.	

liù qīn bú rèn
六親不認
Turn one's back on one's own flesh and blood.

Cut loose from old ties.

例句　Dick married a rich widow and **turned his back on his own flesh and blood**.

出處　老子·六親注："父子兄弟夫婦也。"

同義：視如路人　Cut one dead.	
反義：拉關係　Scrape acquaintance with	

fēn miǎo bì zhēng
分秒必爭
Every minute counts.

Improve each shining hour.

Improve every moment.

 We must hurry up to get to the airport in time, **every minute counts**.

> 同義：一萬年太久，只爭朝夕
> Never put off till tomorrow what may be done today.

> 反義：虛度時光　Kick one's heels.

fēn tíng kàng lǐ
分庭抗禮
As one's rival.

Keep at arm's length.
At loggerheads with

 This product shares the market with that one **as its rival**.

出處 莊子・漁父："萬乘之主，千乘之君，未嘗不分庭伉禮。"

> 同義：大相徑庭　At odds with

fēn dào yáng biāo
分道揚鑣
To part company.

Go separate ways.

 The friends **parted company** because their difference in interests.

同義：各行其是　Have one's own way.
反義：異途同歸　All roads lead to Rome.

huà xiǎn wéi yí
化險為夷
Weather the storm.

Keep one's head above water.
Escape scotfree.
Fall on one's feet.
Bear a charmed life.
To be out of the woods.

 The bankrupted company got a loan to **weather the storm** and reopened.

同義：絕處逢生　Escape by the skin of one's teeth.
反義：晴天霹靂　A bolt from the blue.

fǎn fù wú cháng
反覆無常
Blow hot and cold.

Play fast and loose.

例
句 ▪▪ One should not **blow hot and cold** with what one has promised.

出
處 ▪▪ 漢書："齊夸詐多變，反覆之國。"

同義：風派
The wind keeps not always at one quarter.
反義：始終不渝　Stick to it.

tiān xià wú nán shì　zhǐ pà yǒu xīn rén
天下無難事，只怕有心人
It's dogged that does it.

Where there's a will there's a way.

I am sure that with your determination, you will success. **It's dogged that does it**.

> **反義**：謀事在人，成事在天
>
> Man does what he can, and God what he will.

---

tiān shēng wǒ cái bì yǒu yòng
天生我才必有用
All things in their being are good for something.

Everything is good for something.

 I don't think that I can't take the job because I believe that **all things in their being are good for something**.

> **反義**：朽木不可雕
>
> You cannot make a Mercury of every log.

---

tiān yǒu bú cè zhī fēng yún
天有不測之風雲
Though the sun shines, leave not your cloak at home.

A bolt out of the blue.

You better save some money for the future, **though the sun shines, leave not your cloak at home**, you know!

> **同義：**白雲蒼狗
>
> It is the unforseen that always happens.

成語故事：There's many a slip between the cup and the lip

四畫

舉杯飲酒只是片刻之間的事情，但在這片刻之間都會發生很多意外之事。這是常用以指"世事無常"的成語，典於希臘神話。「阿爾戈船英雄紀」（T h e Argonautica）中的舵手安凱奧斯（Ancacus）不信先知預言說他未能飲到葡萄園中取得的酒就會去世。他嘲笑先知說他已取得葡萄園的酒。先知說：There's many a slip between the cup and the lip。當時有使者來報說他的葡萄園已被野豬踐踏破壞。他沒有喝酒就趕去趕野豬，結果被野豬殺死。

tiān yī wú fèng

天衣無縫

Without a flaw.

Suit one down to the ground.
Fit like a glove.
Fit to a T.

例句 ■ ■ As the old saying points out: Nothing is **without a flaw**.

出處 ■ ■ 靈怪錄：＂有人冉冉自空而下，曰，吾織女也。徐覘其衣，無縫。＂

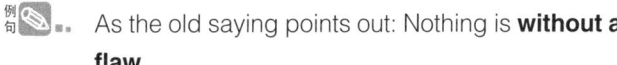

同義：十全十美　The pink of perfection.

tiān yá hǎi jiǎo

天涯海角

Out-of-the-way places.

Ends of the earth.
The uttermost part of the earth.

例句 ■ ■ John said to Jean that he would flow her to **out-of-the way places**.

出處 ■ ■ 游宦記聞：＂今之遠宦及遠服賈者，皆云天涯海角，蓋言遠也。＂

反義：近在咫尺 Within calling distance.

---

tiān wǎng huī huī　shū ér bú lòu

天網恢恢，疏而不漏

Heaven's vengeance is slow but sure.

God's mill grinds slow but sure.
Justice has long arms.
Murder will out.

例句 ▪▪ The corrupted official was caught at last, **heaven's vengeance is slow but sure**.

出處 ▪▪ 老子："天網恢恢，疏而不失。"

---

shào bù gēng shì

少不更事

As green as grass.

Not dry behind the ears.
A green horn.
Born yesterday.

例句 ▪▪ Don't blame the boy for a fault; he is still **as green as grass**.

隋書 · 李雄傳："上謂雄曰,吾兒既少,更事未多。"

> **反義：**老成練達　To have cut one's eyeteeth.

shào zhuàng bù nǔ lì lǎo dà tú shāng bēi
少壯不努力,老大徒傷悲
Rejoiced at in youth, repented in age.

Make the most of one's time.
If you lie upon roses when young, you'll lie upon
　　thorns when old.
Reckless youth makes rueful age.
An idle youth, a needy age.

 The old beggar regretted and quoted the old
saying: **Rejoiced at in youth, repented in age**.

 漢樂府 · 長歌行："百川東到海,何時復西歸,少壯
不努力,老大徒傷悲。"

xīn kǒu rú yī
心口如一
What the heart thinks the tongue speaks.

Mean what one says.
Practice what one preaches.

A promise is a promise, **what the heart thinks the tongue speaks**.

> **同義：**由衷之言　From the bottom of one's heart.

> **反義：**口是心非
> Speak with one's tongue in one's cheek.

xīn bú zài yān
心不在焉
Out to lunch.

To be wool gathering.
To be day-dreaming.
To be absent minded.
A brown study.
Jump the track.

四
畫

 It's no use to speak to a person whose mind is **out to lunch**.

 禮記‧大學："心不在焉，視而不見，聽而不聞，食而不知其味。"

> **同義：**神不守舍　Lose one's presence of mind.

> **反義：**全神貫注　Focus one's attention on.

xīn píng qì hé

心平氣和

Keep cool.

Compose oneself.
Cool as a cucumber.

 When you are challenged, you must **keep cool** before you take any action.

 蘇軾・菜羹賦：〝先生心平而氣和，故雖老而體胖。〞

同義：平心靜氣　Keep one's shirt on.
反義：怒氣沖沖　Fuming with anger.

xīn gān qíng yuàn

心甘情願

With good cheer.

Of one's own accord.
On one's own initiative or free will.

 He gave all he had to her **with good cheer**.

xīn ān lǐ dé
心安理得
Have an easy conscience.

Feel justified.
Have the peace of mind.

例句 ▪▪ Do the right thing to **have an easy conscience**.

出處 ▪▪ 論語："則心安而德全矣。"

同義：問心無愧 Have a clear conscience.
反義：內心慚疚 The prick of conscience.

四
畫

xīn yǒu yú ér lì bù zú
心有餘而力不足
The spirit is willing, but the flesh is weak.

Old bees yield no honey.
Bite off more than one can chew.

例句 ▪▪ He can not fulfil the job because although **the spirit is willing, the flesh is weak**.

同義：力不從心 Beyond one's tether.
反義：餘勇可賈 Enough and to spare.

xīn zhí kǒu kuài
心直口快

Nearest the heart, nearest the mouth.

What the heart thinks the tongue speaks.
Frank and out-spoken.

例句 ■■ An open-minded man speaks openly as the **nearest the heart, nearest the month**.

出處 ■■ 元曲選‧張國賓‧羅李郎：＂哥哥是心直口快射糧軍。＂

同義：知無不言，言無不盡　Lay one's heart bare.

反義：支吾其詞　To hum and haw.

---

xīn huā nù fàng
心花怒放

Burst with joy.

One's heart sings with joy.
To be in one's glory.

例句 ■■ When he heard the good news, he **bursted with joy**.

出處 ■■ 梁‧簡文帝：＂心花成樹，共轉六塵。＂

反義：悶悶不樂　Eat one's heart out.

xīn yuán yì mǎ
心猿意馬
Run with the hound and hold with the hare.

Carry fire in one hand and water in the other.

例
句　　If you **run with the hound and hold with the hare**,
you can never make a right choice.

出
處　　參同契注：「心猿不定，意馬四馳。」

xīn mǎn yì zú
心滿意足
Pat oneself on the back.

To one's heart's content.
After one's own heart.
Rest on one's laurels.
Warm the cockles of one's heart.
Look like the cat that ate (swallowed) the canary.

例
句　　John **patted himself on the back** for the record
he had made in the race.

同義：如願以償　To have one's will.

---

xīn kuàng shén yí
心曠神怡
In fine fettle.

Feel on top of the world.
Get out of bed on the right side.
In good spirit.

 The poet was **in fine fettle** when he was reciting his own poems.

 宋・范仲淹・岳陽樓記："心曠神怡，寵辱皆忘。"

---

xīn jīng dǎn zhàn
心驚膽戰
Tremble (shake) like a leaf.

Tremble with fear.
To be panic stricken.
Get cold feet.
Have one's heart in one's mouth.
Push the panic button.
Send a chill down one's spine.

The child **trembled like a leaf** while listening to the ghost story.

> **同義：**不寒而慄　Make one's teeth chatter.

zhī wú qí cí
支吾其詞
To hem and haw.

To hum and ha.
Speak with one's tongue in one's cheek.
To falter one's words.

 He **hemmed and hawed** to answer that hasty question.

史記："諸將皆懾伏，無敢枝梧。"

> **同義：**含糊其詞　Beat about the bush.

> **反義：**心直口快　Nearest the heart, nearest the mouth.

四
畫

wén guò shì fēi
文過飾非
Gloss over faults.

Fine words dress ill deeds.

Varnishing hides a crack.
Speech was given to man to disguise his thoughts.
To whitewash something.

 A few fine words may **gloss over faults** but can not covers the losses.

 唐・劉知幾・史通・惑經："庸儒末學，文過飾非。"

> **反義**：知錯認錯
> Confession is the first step to repentence.

jīn jīn jì jiào
斤斤計較
Look at both sides of a penny.

Strain at a gnat.
Skin a flint.

 A miser always **look at both sides of a penny** when he buys something.

同義：錙銖計較　Chase eights and quarters.
反義：滿不在乎　Not to care a pin.

fāng xīng wèi ài
方興未艾
In the bud.

In the ascendant.
On the upgrade.
In infancy.

例句 ■■ The reform was nipped **in the bud**.

同義：欣欣向榮　Flourish like the green bay-tree.

反義：日薄西山　Sinking fast.

四畫

rì yuè rú suō
日月如梭
Time flies like an arrow.

例句 ■■ We have been away for almost ten years, **time flies like an arrow**.

出處 ■■ 宋・趙德璘・侯鯖錄："織鳥，日也，往來如梭之織。"

反義：寸陰若歲　Time hangs heavy on one's hand.

rì jī yuè lěi

日積月累

Accumulated through the year.

Pile-up.
Keep some till more come.

 The man's collection of stamps, **accumulated through the year**, is now worth a fortune.

 顧炎武・日知錄・禁自宮："自是以後，日積月累，千百成羣，其為國之蠹害甚矣。"

同義：銖積寸累　Little and often fills the purse.
反義：一擲千金　Spend money like water.

rì bó xī shān

日薄西山

One's days are numbered.

The sands are running out.
Not to be long for this world.
Sinking fast.

 The **tyrant's days are numbered** with his army's rebellion against him.

出處 李密‧陳情表："今劉日薄西山，氣息奄奄，人命危淺，朝不慮夕。"

同義：行將就木　On one's last legs.

---

mù yǐ chéng zhōu
木已成舟
It's no use crying over spilt milk.

What's done can't be undone.

例句 **It's no use crying over spilt milk** when you overlooked the flaws and bought it.

同義：米已成炊　The die is cast.

反義：初歸新婦，落地孩兒
Train a tree when it is young.

四畫

---

bǐ bǐ jiē shì
比比皆是
Right and left.

Here and there and everywhere.

Such items can be found **right and left**, at lower prices, too.

 明‧陶宗儀‧輟耕錄：〝朝為師生而暮若途人者，比比皆是。〞

同義：滿坑滿谷　As thick as blackberries.
反義：寥若晨星　Few and far between.

máo gǔ sǒng rán
毛骨悚然
Make one's flesh creep.

Make one creep all over.
Make one's hair stand on end.
Get goose bumps.

 The news about the massacre **made one's flesh creep**.

同義：不寒而慄　Make one's teeth chatter.

shuǐ xiè bù tōng

水洩不通

Packed like sardines.

To be chock-a-block.

例句  All types of vehicles **packed like sardines** during rush hours along this road.

出處 釋道源・景德傳燈錄：〝德山門下，水洩不通。〞

> **反義**：川流不息　In rapid succession.

shuǐ shēn huǒ rè

水深火熱

Go through fire and water.

Get into hot water.
Hard in a clinch and no knife to cut the seizing.
To be in deep water.

例句 He will **go through fire and water** to do it for you.

出處 孟子・梁惠王下：〝如水益深，如火益熱。〞

shuǐ luò shí chū

水落石出

Brought to light.

Truth lies at the bottom of a well.
The truth will out.
To come out in the wash.
Murder is out.

例句 ✎ ▪ The mystery is **brought to light** at last.

出處 ✎ ▪ 蘇軾・後赤壁賦：〝山高月小，水落石出。〞

同義：真相大白　Everything comes to light.

shuǐ dī shí chuān

水滴石穿

By sheer strength of will.

Constant dripping of water wears away the stone.
Little strokes fell great oaks.
Hair and hair makes the man's head bare.
Drop by drop the sea is drained.

例句 ✎ ▪ Nothing can not be accomplished **by sheer strength of will**.

出處 漢書‧枚乘傳：“繩鋸木斷，水滴石穿。”

> **同義**：繩鋸木斷
>
> Feather by feather the goose is plucked.

huǒ shàng jiā yóu

火上加油

Pour oil on the flame (fire).

Add fuel to the flames.
Like a red rag to a bull.

四
畫

例句 To put the blame on an angry person is to **pour oil on the flame**.

出處 元曲選‧陳州糶米：“我從來不劣方頭，恰便是火上澆油。”

> **同義**：推波助瀾　Fan the fire.

> **反義**：釜底抽薪
>
> Take away fuel, take away flame (fire).

yǐ xiǎo rén zhī xīn duó jūn zǐ zhī fù
以小人之心度君子之腹
A rogue always suspects deceit.

 He always speaks ill of others because **a rogue always suspects deceit**.

 世説新語：" 可謂以小人之慮，度君子之心。"

> **同義：**以己度人
> Measure another's corn by one's own bushel.

yǐ luǎn jī shí
以卵擊石
Throw a straw against the wind.

Run one's head against a stone wall.
Whether the pitcher strikes the stone, or the stone the pitcher, it is bad for the pitcher.

 For a small company to compete with a giant one, it is to **throw a straw against the wind**.

 墨子・貴義：" 以其言非吾言者，是猶以卵投石也。"

> **同義：**螳臂擋車　Kick against the pricks.

yǐ shēn zuò zé

以身作則

Practice what you preach.

Set a good example for others.

 You have to **practice what you preach** so that your students will follow you.

同義：身教勝於言教 Example is better than precept.
反義：好話説盡，壞事做盡 The devil can cite Scripture for his purpose.

五畫

yǐ yuàn bào dé

以怨報德

Bite the hand that feeds one.

Return evil for good.
The axe goes to the wood where it borrowed its helve.
Save a thief from the gallows and he will cut your throat.

 It is mean to **bite the hand that feeds one**.

反義：以德報怨　Return good for evil.

yǐ yǎn huán yǎn yǐ yá huán yá
以眼還眼，以牙還牙
Pay one back in his own coin.

An eye for an eye; a tooth for a tooth.
Return like for like.
Tit for tat.
Give as good as one gets (takes).

 John refused to support Robert, **paying him back in his own coin** because he had been refused by Robert for support.

> **同義：**針鋒相對　Measure for measure.

zhàng shì qī rén
仗勢欺人
Pull rank on someone.

Throw one's weight about.

 The boss **pulled rank on Robert** by asking him to prepare tea for guests.

 明·李開先·林沖寶劍記："賊子無知，仗勢欺人敢妄為。"

> **同義：**盛氣凌人　Throw one's weight about.

zhàng yì shū cái

仗義疏財

Come down handsome.

Tip the brads.
Be a good Samaritan.
A do-gooder.

He contributed a great sum to the fund, **coming down so handsomely**.

水滸傳傳奇：〝宋公明他扶危濟困隱功曹，晁保正他疏財仗義豪。〞

| **同義：**扶危濟困　Help a lame dog over a stile. |
| **反義：**一毛不拔　As tight as a drum. |

五畫

chōng ěr bù wén

充耳不聞

None so deaf as those who won't hear.

Turn a deaf ear to

The boss took no advice from us as **none so deaf as those who won't listen**.

詩經：〝叔兮伯兮，褎如充耳。〞

> **同義**：耳邊風　In at one ear and out at the other.
>
> **反義**：洗耳恭聽　To be all ears.

chū rén tóu dì
出人頭地

To be head and shoulders taller.

Come to the fore.

例句 ▪▪ John **is head and shoulder taller** in his class.

出處 ▪▪ 宋史："吾當避此人出一頭地。"

> **同義**：不亞於人　Second to none.
>
> **反義**：無地自容　To be put out of countenance.

chū kǒu chéng zhāng
出口成章

One's tongue is the pen of a ready writer.

例句 ▪▪ A good **speaker's tongue is the pen of a ready writer**.

蘇軾文："脫口成章，粲莫可耘。"

> **反義：**張口結舌　At a loss for words.

chū wū ní ér bù rǎn
出污泥而不染
Lilies are whitest in a blackamoor's hand.

 He was brought up in slum and became president of the firm, **lilies are whitest in a blackamoor's hand**.

 宋・周敦頤・愛蓮說："余獨愛蓮之出污泥而不染，濯清漣而不妖，中通外直，不蔓不枝。"

> **反義：**染於蒼則蒼，染於黃則黃
> Touch pitch, and you will be defiled.

五畫

chū yán bú xùn
出言不遜
Put one's foot in one's mouth.

Drop a clanger.

 Forgive his rude remarks, he is used to **put his foot in his mouth**.

出處 ■ 三國志・魏志・張郃傳："郃快軍敗，出言不遜。"

> **同義：**大放厥詞　To let oneself loose.

chū qí zhì shèng
出奇制勝
To outwit.

Take by surprise.
To cope with

例句 ■ You **outwitted** John and won the prize.

出處 ■ 史記："兵以正合，出奇制勝，善之者出其無窮。"

> **同義：**智取為上
> Contrivance is better than force.

chū ěr fǎn ěr
出爾反爾
Play fast and loose.

Blow hot and cold.
Go back on one's word.

例句 ▪▪ Be true to what you have promised and do not **play fast and loose**.

出處 ▪▪ 孟子：〝戒之戒之，出乎爾者，反乎爾者也。〞

同義：朝令夕改 The law is not the same at morning and night.

反義：一言為定　A bargain is a bargain.

chū lèi bá cuì
出類拔萃
Tower above the rest.

Out of the common run.
In a class by itself.
Distinguish oneself.

例句 ▪▪ In his trade, John **towers above the rest**.

出處 ▪▪ 孟子：〝出於其類，拔乎其萃。〞

同義：卓爾不羣　Come to the fore.

反義：平平庸庸　Pass in a crowd in a push.

五畫

gōng bài chuí chéng
功敗垂成

A slip betwixt the cup and the lip.

A flash in the pan.

例句 ■ Tom is disqualified at the final round, **a slip betwixt the cup and the lip**.

出處 ■ 漢書:"垂成之功,敗於一日。"

> **同義**:功虧一簣　Look back from the plough.

> **反義**:一蹴而就　At one stroke.

gōng kuī yí kuì
功虧一簣

Give up when near success.

Look back from the plough.
Another course would have done it.

例句 ■ Regrettable to see that you **give up when near success**.

出處 ■ 尚書・旅獒:"為山九仞,功虧一簣。"

> **反義**:大功告成　Come off with honours.

bàn tú ér fèi

半途而廢

Do things by halves.

Drop (fall) by the wayside.
Not go the whole hog.

例句 ■■ It is silly to **do things by halves**.

出處 ■■ 禮記：＂君子遵道而行，半途而廢，吾弗能已矣。＂

> **反義**：堅持到底　Stick it out.

sī kōng jiàn guàn

司空見慣

Order of the day.

Par for the course.

例句 ■■ Such practices are the **order of the day**.

出處 ■■ 劉禹錫詩：＂司空見慣渾閑事，斷盡蘇州刺史腸。＂

> **同義**：比比皆是　Right and left.

> **反義**：千載難逢
> It only happens once in a blue moon.

五畫

lìng yǎn xiāng kàn

另眼相看

Regard with favour.

See in a new light.

 Tom is **regarded with favour** by his supervisor.

> **同義**：士別三日，刮目相看
> Wanton kittens may make sober cats.

> **反義**：一視同仁　When it rains it rains on all alike.

sì fēn wǔ liè

四分五裂

To be torn asunder.

Fall apart.
Break up.

 The country **is torn asunder** in the revolution.

漢書："此四分五裂之國也。"

> **反義**：團結一致　To hang together.

sì píng bā wěn

四平八穩

As firm as a rock.

On the safe side.
On all fours.
Play safe.
Safe and sure.

 The company stands **as firm as a rock** during the inflation.

> 反義：鋌而走險　Run a risk.

五
畫

sì miàn bā fāng

四面八方

Here, there and everywhere.

Length and breadth.
Far and wide.
High and low.
In all directions.
Right and left.
Here and there.

Tourists come from **here, there and everywhere** to visit Beijing.

釋道源·景德傳燈錄：〝忽遇四面八方怎麼生。〞

sì hǎi wéi jiā
四海為家
Here today and gone tomorrow.

 He travelled around places, **here today and gone tomorrow**.

 漢書·高帝紀：〝天子以四海為家。〞

sì tōng bā dá
四通八達
Within easy reach.

There are more ways to the wood than one.

 The city is **within easy reach**, at the hub of the country.

 子華子·晏子問黨：〝其途之所出，四通而八達。〞

> **反義：**死胡同　A blind alley.

shī zhī dōng yú   shōu zhī sāng yú
失之東隅，收之桑榆
Lose in hake but gain in herring.

What one loses on the swings, one gains on the
　　roundabouts.
Get in the shire what one loses in the hundred.

例句　He lost money in the stock market but won in the
　　horserace – **lose in hake but gain in herring**.

出處　後漢書‧馮異傳："始雖垂翅回溪，終能奮翼澠池，
　　可謂失之東隅，收之桑榆。"

> **反義：**賠了夫人又折兵
> 　　Throw the helve after the hatchet.

五
畫

shī bài nǎi chéng gōng zhī mǔ
失敗乃成功之母
Learn by experience.

Failure teaches success.

例句　Never give up and remember that success is to
　　learn by experience.

> **同義：**吃一塹，長一智
> 　　Experience is the mother of wisdom.

qiǎo fù nán wéi wú mǐ zhī chuī

巧婦難為無米之炊

Bear walls make giddy housewives.

You cannot make bricks without straw.
With empty hands men may no hawks lure.
What's a workman without his tools?

例句 ▪▪ To cover all expenses with so little fund is what we called: **Bare walls make giddy housewives**.

出處 ▪▪ 陸游 · 老學庵筆記： "巧婦安能作無麵湯餅乎。"

zuǒ zhī yòu chù

左支右絀

Can't make both ends meet.

To be in a tight squeeze.

例句 ▪▪ He **can't make both ends meet** with what he is getting from his work.

出處 ▪▪ 清 · 紀昀 · 閱微草堂筆記： "左支右絀，困不可忍。"

同義：手頭拮据 To be hard up.
反義：一擲千金 Spend money like water.

zuǒ yòu féng yuán

左右逢源

Everything goes well.

It is good to have friends both in heaven and in hell.

例句 ■■ He has many friends in that city and **everything goes well** for him to do business there.

出處 ■■ 孟子・離婁下：〝資之深，則取之左右逢其原。〞

同義：八面玲瓏　All things to all men.
反義：進退維谷　On the horns of a dilemma.

五畫

píng fēn qiū sè

平分秋色

On equal terms with

Share and share alike.
Go fifty-fifty.

例句 ■■ We are **on equal terms with** other shareholders to get our bonus.

出處 ■■ 李樸・中秋詩：〝平分秋色一輪滿，長伴雲衢千里明。〞

同義：二一添作五　Go halves.
反義：多吃多佔　Take the lion share.

píng bù qīng yún

平 步 青 雲

Skyrocket to fame.

Hit the jackpot.

To have crept through the hawsehole.

Beat the top of the ladder (tree).

Come to the top over night.

Make a smashing hit.

例句 ■· John has **skyrocketed to fame** after the publication of his latest book.

出處 ■· 曹鄴詩："一旦公道開，青雲在平地。"

同義：飛黃騰達　Rise in the world.
反義：一落千丈　To go to pot.

běn mò dào zhì

本末倒置

Put the cart before the horse.

Turn topsy-turvy.

 Writing a book review before you have read the whole book is **putting the cart before the horse**.

大學："物有本末，事有終始。"

同義：冠履倒置 Turn things upside down.
反義：撥亂反正 Put things back to order.

五畫

wèi yǔ chóu móu

未雨綢繆

Make hay while the sun shines.

Strike while the iron is hot.
Lay up against a rainy day.
In fair weather prepare for foul.
Though the sun shines, leave not your cloak at home.

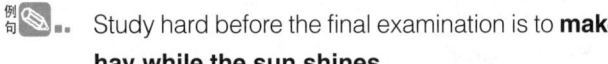 Study hard before the final examination is to **make hay while the sun shines**.

出處 ■■ 詩經・豳風・鴟鴞： "迨天之未陰雨，徹彼桑土，綢繆牖戶。"

> **同義**：防患未然　Take precaution.

> **反義**：平時不燒香，急時抱佛腳
> Once on shore, we pray no more.

zhèng zhòng xià huái
正中下懷
After one's own heart.

To one's liking.

例句 ■■ Thank you for the gift which is just **after my own heart**.

> **同義**：先獲我心　Prepossess one favourably.

> **反義**：討厭萬分　Bored to death.

gān zhī rú yí
甘之如飴
Smack one's lips.

With relish.

Lick one's chops.

例句 :: Tom tasted the dish and **smacked his lips**, saying: "Yummy!"

出處 :: 文天祥・正氣歌："鼎鑊甘如飴，求之不可得。"

同義：津津有味　With gusto.
反義：苦不堪言　As bitter as gall.

gān bài xià fēng
甘拜下風
Eat humble pie.

Lower one's flag.
Play second fiddle.
Take a back seat.
To sit at a person's feet.

例句 :: He is willing to **eat humble pie** under that scholar after reading his book.

出處 :: 左傳・僖十五年："皇天后土，實聞君之言，羣臣敢在下風。"

反義：不甘後人　Not to be outdone.

shēng qì bó bó

生氣勃勃

Full of vitality.

Full of vim and vigor.
Full of pep (life).
To be alive and kicking.

 A person **full of vitality** may join the rescue team.

 鍾嶸詩品："袁蝦云，我詩有生氣，須人捉著，不
爾便飛去。"

> **反義**：暮氣沉沉　Lose one's grip.

shēng lóng huó hǔ

生龍活虎

Alive and kicking.

Look as if one has eaten live birds.
Brimming over with life.

 He has recovered from illness and is now **alive
and kicking**.

> **同義**：蹦蹦跳跳　Jump like parched peas.

> **反義**：呆若木雞　To be rooted to the spot.

bái shǒu qǐ jiā

白手起家

Start from scratch.

A self-made man.

 Tom established his business, **started from scratch**.

> **反義：**家道中落　To be worse off.

bái rì zuò mèng

白日作夢

To be day-dreaming.

In a brown study.

 You **are day-dreaming** if you think you can get a diamond ring at that price.

> **同義：**想入非非　Build castles in the air.

> **反義：**頭腦清醒　To be all there.

五
畫

mù bù jiāo jié

目不交睫

To be wide awake.

To be all alert.

 I **was wide awake** last night after reading that detective story.

同義：金睛火眼　Keep one's eyes skinned.
反義：昏昏欲睡　Have a wink in one's eye.

mù bù zhuǎn jīng

目不轉睛

Fix one's eyes on.

One's eyes are riveted on (glued to)
Keep one's best eye peeled.

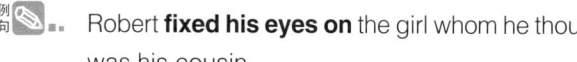 Robert **fixed his eyes on** the girl whom he thought was his cousin.

mù bù shí dīng

目不識丁

An illiterate.

Not to know A from a windmill.
Not to know B from a bull's foot.

例句 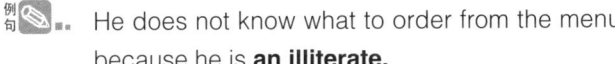 He does not know what to order from the menu because he is **an illiterate.**

出處 新唐書‧張宏靖傳："天下無事，爾輩挽兩石弓，不如識一丁字。"

同義：胸無點墨 A numskull.
反義：博學多才 Know a thing or two.

五畫

mù kōng yí qiè

目空一切

View everyone with a scornful eye.

Turn a blind eye to
Have one's nose in the air.
As proud as a peacock.

例句 Having been promoted to a higher position, Robert **viewed everyone with a scornful eye**.

| 同義：唯我獨尊 | To be overweening. |

| 反義：妄自菲薄 | Make oneself too cheap. |

jiāo tóu jiē ěr
交頭接耳
To bill and coo.

Head to head.
Have a tête à tête with

例句 Jack and Jill sat there **billing and cooing** like a pair of love birds.

出處 水滸傳："他那三四個交頭接耳說話。"

yǎng rén bí xī
仰人鼻息
To be under one's thumb.

Live on the charity of
To be led by the nose.
Consult one's pleasure.

At somebody's mercy.

例句 ■■ The sergeant had had the second lieutenant **under his thumb** ever since he learned of the lieutenant's past.

出處 ■■ 後漢書·袁紹傳：〝袁紹孤客窮軍，仰我鼻息。〞

> **反義：**頤指氣使　Get someone by the short hairs.

guāng míng lěi luò
光明磊落
To be open and aboveboard.

As clear as crystal.

例句 ■■ A gentleman's activities **are open and aboveboard**.

出處 ■■ 晉書：〝大丈夫行為，當磊磊落落，如日月皎然。〞

> **同義：**胸懷坦蕩　As open as the day.

> **反義：**鬼鬼祟祟　Up to some hangky-pangky.

guāng yīn sì jiàn
光陰似箭
How time flies.

Time flies like an arrow.

 To see the children off to study abroad, Mrs. Jones sensed **how time flies**.

 韋莊 · 關河道中詩 : "但見時光流似箭,豈知天道曲如弓。"

xiān fā zhì rén
先發制人
To anticipate the enemy.

Steal a march on one.
Get the jump (drop) on one.
Catch the ball before the bound.
Steal one's thunder.
Take the wind out of one's sails.

 To anticipate the enemy is to win the battle.

 漢書 · 項籍傳 : "先發制人,後發制於人。"

> **同義:**先下手為強　Forestall the enemy.

quán lì yǐ fù

全力以赴

To go all out.

Go at it hammer and tongs.
To work up to the collar.
Put the best foot (leg) forward (foremost).
Put one's shoulder to the wheel.
With might and main.

 The rescue team **went all out** to save the people out of the fire.

同義：不遺餘力　Tooth and nail.
反義：袖手旁觀　Stand by with folded arms.

quán xīn quán yì

全心全意

Heart and soul.

Set one's mind on.

 He always does his job with **heart and soul**.

反義：半心半意　Half heart is no heart.

quán shén guàn zhù

全神貫注

Zero in on

Focus one's attention on
Concentrate upon
Sink one's teeth into

例句 ■■ The president **zeroed in on** taxes for the year.

同義：專心致志　With undivided attention.
反義：心不在焉　To be wool-gathering.

zài jiē zài lì

再接再厲

Redouble one's efforts.

Make unremitting efforts.

例句 ■■ Tom **redoubled his efforts** to accomplish the project.

出處 ■■ 韓愈 · 鬥雞聯句： "一噴一醒然，再接再厲乃。"

同義：百尺竿頭，更進一步　Make further efforts.
反義：一蹶不振　Fall flat.

bīng dòng sān chǐ　fēi yí rì zhī hán
冰凍三尺，非一日之寒
Ill habits gather by unseen degrees.

The tree falls not at the first stroke.
An oak is not felled at one stroke.

例句 ✐ ▪▪ Smoking caused the man lung cancer as **ill habits gather by unseen degrees**.

wěn jǐng zhī jiāo
刎頸之交
Damon and Pythias.

例句 ✐ ▪▪ Jack and John are **Damon and Pythias**.

出處 ✐ ▪▪ 史記 · 廉頗藺相如列傳："卒相與歡，為刎頸之交。"

> **同義**：莫逆之交　A sworn friend.

> **反義**：不共戴天之仇　Deadly feud.

wēi zài dàn xī
危在旦夕
Hang on by the eyelids (one's eyelashes).

Sword of Damocles.

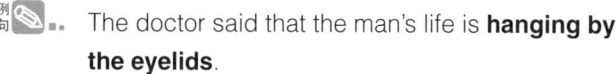

例句 ■■ The doctor said that the man's life is **hanging by the eyelids**.

出處 ■■ 三國志 · 吳志 · 太史慈傳："今管亥暴亂,北海(孔融)被圍,孤窮無援,危在旦夕。"

同義:火燒眉毛　Imminent danger.
反義:安如泰山　Safe upon the solid rock.

tóng xīn xié lì

同心協力

Make common cause.

Pull together.
Pool efforts.
Unite as one.

例句 ■■ We all do our best and **make the job our common cause**.

出處 ■■ 三國演義:"我三人結為兄弟,協力同心,然後可圖大事。"

同義:戮力同心　To hang together.
反義:各行其是　Have one's own way.

tóng gān gòng kǔ

同甘共苦

Friendships multiply joys and divide griefs.

A sorrow shared is but half a trouble, but a joy that is shared is a joy made double.
In weal or woe.

例
句 ▪▪ We help each other and feel that **friendships multiply joys and divide grief**.

出
處 ▪▪ 晉書·應詹傳：「詹與分甘共苦，情若兄弟。」

> **同義**：有福同享，有禍同當
> For better or for worse.

> **反義**：有酒有肉多兄弟，急難何曾見一人
> In tlme ot prosperity friends will be plenty; in time of adversity not one among twenty.

六畫

tóng zhōu gòng jì

同舟共濟

Company in distress makes sorrow less.

He that pities another remembers himself.

Tom and John put their money together to cover the loss as **company in distress makes sorrow less**.

 孫子・九地：〝夫吳人與越人相惡也，當其同舟而濟，遇風，其相救也，若左右手。〞

反義：各自打算　Strike out for oneself.

---

tóng liú hé wū
同流合污

Birds of a feather flock together.

Act in collusion with
Wallow in the mire with
Play into one another's hands.

 They are always together to get drunk as **birds of a feather flock together**.

 孟子・盡心下：〝同乎流俗，合乎污世。〞

同義：朋比為奸　Gang up with

反義：潔身自好
　　　　Better be alone than in bad company.

---

tóng bìng xiāng lián

同病相憐

In the same boat.

Two in distress make trouble less.
Misery loves company.
Misery acquaints a man with strange bedfellows.
Company in distress makes sorrow less.
He that pities another remembers himself.

 I am not the only person who has this problem.
Several women I know are **in the same boat**.

 吳越春秋 · 闔閭內傳："同病相憐，同憂相救。"

同義：患難之交　Foul weather friends.
反義：漠不關心　Devil-may-care.

六畫

gè rén zì sǎo mén qián xuě

各人自掃門前雪

Sweep before your own door.

Let each tailor mend his own coat.
Let every man skin his own skunk.
Let everyone mind his own business.

Selfishness makes you **sweep before your own door** after snowing.

> **同義：**事不關己，高高掛起
> Dogs never go into mourning when a horse dies.

> **反義：**通力合作　To pull together.

gè dé qí suǒ
各得其所

A place for everything, and everything in its place.

 John won the prize and Tom got the scholarship – **a place for everything, and everything in it's place**.

 周易 • 繫辭下："交易而退，各得其所。"

> **同義：**得其所哉　Fall into place.

> **反義：**不得其所　Out of place.

gè shì qí shì

各適其適

One man's meat is another man's poison.

A barley corn is better than a diamond to a cock.
Jack Sprat could eat no fat; and his wife could eat
　　no lean; and so betwixt them both, you see, they
　　lick the platter clean.

例句 ✎ ▪▪ I don't see what you see in that girl, **one man's
meat is another man's poison**.

míng bù xū chuán

名不虛傳

Live up to one's reputation.

Worthy of the name.

例句 ✎ ▪▪ You have to read his book to understand that the
writer is **living up to his reputation**.

出處 ✎ ▪▪ 北史：〝名下固無虛士也。〞

反義：徒有虛名　To be a figurehead.

六
畫

míng liè qián máo

名列前茅

Head the list.

Come to the fore.
Bear away the bell.
Carry everything before one.
Take the cake.

例句 Jim always **heads the list** in his class.

同義：獨佔鰲頭　Come out first.
反義：倒數第一　To bring up the rear.

míng chuí qiān gǔ

名垂千古

Their names liveth for evermore.

例句 Heros in the history passed away, but **their names liveth for evermore**.

出處 蘇頲文："流譽千古。"

同義：永垂不朽　Go down to posterity.
反義：身敗名裂　Die like a dog.

míng fù qí shí

名副其實

To be worthy of one's name.

In every sense of the word.

 Read his book and you'll see that he **is worthy of his name** as a great writer.

同義：名不虛傳	Live up to one's reputation.
反義：虛有其名	A rope of sand.

míng luò sūn shān

名落孫山

Get plucked.

Take a plough.
To be ploughed.
Flunk and exam.

 He **gets plucked** in the final examination.

 范公偁‧過庭錄："孫山曰，解名盡處是孫山，賢郎更落孫山外。"

反義：獨佔鰲頭	Carry off the palm.

六
畫

míng zào yì shí
名噪一時

To rise to fame.

Make a noise in the world.

例句 ■■ The debut was so successful that it made the actress **to rise to fame**.

出處 ■■ 唐書：「即授太子正字，公卿邀請旁午，號神童，名震一時。」

> **反義**：名譽掃地　Fall into disgrace.

yīn xiǎo shī dà
因小失大

Lose a ship for a halfpenny worth of tar.

例句 ■■ It is to **lose a ship for a halfpenny worth of tar** if you do not buy the travel insurance.

出處 ■■ 呂氏春秋：「達子請金齊王以賞軍，齊王怒不給……及戰大敗……此貪於小利以失大利者也。」

> **同義**：貪他一斗米，失卻半年糧
> Many go out for wool and come back shorn.

成語故事：Never spoil a ship for a haporth of tar

此諺直譯：不要為了半分錢損害一隻船。Haporth為英國口語，意為halfpenny worth（值半便士），在此語中喻微量。船漏水，要塗柏油（tar）防漏。為了捨不得小量的柏油，結果損失了船，正是我們說的因小失大。日本諺語有相應者作：惜一文而不知百事。一說這是英國古老諺語，原來句中的ship是sheep，因為從前羊受了傷是用柏塗治的。十九世紀期間人們將sheep改作ship，據說和英國航運發達有關。

yīn xún shǒu jiù

因循守舊

Follow the beaten track.

Stick-in-the-mud.

例句 No reform may be expected by **following the beaten track**.

同義：墨守成規　To move in a rut.

六畫

duō duō yì shàn
多多益善
The more the better.

All is fish that comes to his net.
All's grist that comes to the mill.

例句 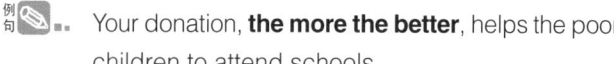 Your donation, **the more the better**, helps the poor children to attend schools.

出處 史記‧淮陰侯傳:"上問曰,如我能將幾何,信曰,不過十萬,上曰,於君何如,曰,臣多多益善耳。"

wàng zì zūn dà
妄自尊大
Full of conceit.

Think no small beer of oneself.
A fly on the coach wheel.
Grow too big for one's boots.

例句 The man was **full of conceit** when he said that he is in a position to control the situation.

出處 後漢書‧馬援傳:"子陽(公孫述字)井底蛙耳,而妄自尊大。"

同義：夜郎自大
　　　Every sprat nowadays calls itself herring.

反義：自慚形穢　Have an inferiority complex.

wàng zì fěi bó
妄自菲薄
A sense of inferiority.

Make oneself too cheap.

例句■ Nothing can be accomplished by a person with **a sense of inferiority**.

出處■ 諸葛亮・出師表：「不宜妄自菲薄，引喻失義，以塞忠諫之路也。」

同義：自暴自棄　Stand in one's own light.

反義：夜郎自大　To be full of oneself.

六畫

hào gāo wù yuǎn
好高騖遠
Hitch one's wagon to a star.

Gaze at the moon and fall into the gutter.

Vaulting ambition that overleaps itself.

 You must not **hitch your wagon to a star** when you make your plan for your future.

同義：想入非非　To be in the clouds.
反義：腳踏實地　Come down to bedrock.

hǎo jǐng bù cháng
好景不常

The morning sun never lasts a day.

The longest day must have an end.
Every day is not Sunday.
A wonder lasts but nine days.

 The social disorder destroyed the once prosperous town, **the morning sun never lasts a day**.

 王勃："好景不常，盛筵難再。"

反義：天下無不散之筵席　Merry meet, merry part.

rú huǒ rú tú

如火如荼

Crop up like mushrooms.

In full blast.
In full swing.

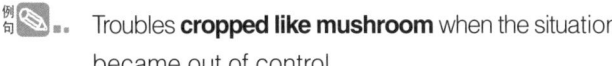 Troubles **cropped like mushroom** when the situation
became out of control.

國語 · 吳語："令萬人以為方陣,皆白裳,……望之
如荼。左軍亦如之,皆赤裳,……望之如火。"

同義:風頭火勢　Like a house afire.
反義:煙消雲散　End in smoke.

rú zuò zhēn zhān

如坐針氈

Sit on thorns.

To be on pins and needles.
To be on tenterhooks.
Lie on a bed of thorns.

Listening to his brags is to **sit on thorns**.

晉書 · 杜錫傳:"置針著錫常所坐處氈中,刺之流血。"

六
畫

| 同義：坐立不安 | Sit on a bag of fleas. |

| 反義：舒舒服服 | As snug as a bug in a rug. |

rú yú dé shuǐ
如魚得水
Feel oneself at home.

Like a duck to water.
To be in one's element.

 John **feels himself at home** with his new job.

 三國志 · 蜀志 · 諸葛亮傳："孤（劉備自稱）之有孔
明，猶魚之有水也。"

| 同義：優哉悠哉 | Free and easy. |

| 反義：涸轍之鮒 | A fish out of water. |

rú mèng chū xǐng
如夢初醒
To wake up to

It dawns upon one.

He lost his money and **waked up to** the fact that he had been cheated.

> 同義：恍然大悟　See daylight.

rú lǚ bó bīng
如履薄冰
Skate on thin ice.

Tread as on eggs.

 You'll be **skating on thin ice** if you press on harder.

出處 詩經·小雅：「戰戰兢兢，如臨深淵，如履薄冰。」

> 同義：小心戒慎　Take heed is a good rede.

> 反義：莽莽撞撞　Like a bull in a china shop.

六畫

rú shǔ jiā zhēn
如數家珍
Know the inside out.

To have at one's fingers' tips (ends).
To cover the waterfront.

例句 ■■ He **knows the fact** **inside out**.

出處 ■■ 韓詩外傳："贈之不與家珍。"

rú jiāo sì qī
如膠似漆
Sticking together.

To be hand and glove with

例句 ■■ Jack and Jean are in love, **sticking together** like a pair of love birds.

出處 ■■ 史記："感於心，合於行，親於膠漆。"

同義：親密無間　They cleave together like burrs.

反義：冰炭不相容
At loggerheads with one another.

---

rú yuàn yǐ cháng
如願以償
The prayer is answered.

Long looked for comes at last.
A dream comes true.

To have one's will.

Bring home the bacon.

例句 ■■ Tom got what he wished, his **prayer is answered**.

出處 ■■ 黃庭堅："政當為公乞如願。"

同義：正中下懷　After one's own heart.

反義：大失所望

Fish for herring and catch a sprat.

---

shǒu kǒu rú píng

守口如瓶

Put a lid on.

Not breathe a word about.

As close as an oyster.

To be a regular oyster.

Keep mum.

Clam up.

Wild horses would not drag it from one.

例句 ■■ Only you and I know the fact and we have to **put a lid on** the secret.

出處 ■■ 周密 · 癸辛雜識："富鄭公有守口如瓶，防意如城之語。"

六畫

同義：三緘其口	One's lips are sealed.
反義：洩漏機密	Let the cat out of the bag.

ān fèn shǒu jǐ
安分守己
Know one's distance.

Know where to draw a line.
Mind one's own business.

例句 ■■ John **knows his distance** and never puts his finger in other person's pie.

出處 ■■ 蘇軾詩："胡不安其份，但聽物所誘。"

同義：循規蹈矩	Walk the chalk.
反義：橫行無忌	Throw one's weight about.

ān rú tài shān
安如泰山
Safe upon the solid rock.

例句 ■■ His position is **safe upon solid rock** after he gave your recommendation letter to his boss.

出處 ▪▪ 文選・枚乘諫吳王書：" 乘所欲為，易於反掌，安於泰山。"

同義：固若金湯　As firm as a rock.

反義：危在旦夕　Hang on by the eyelids.

chéng zé wéi wáng　bài zé wéi kòu
成則為王，敗則為寇
Losers are always in the wrong.

A thief passes for a gentleman when thieving has
　　made him rich.

例句 ▪▪ They are banished by the king after their rebellion,
losers are always in the wrong.

kòu rén xīn xián
扣人心弦
Tug at one's heartstrings.

例句 ▪▪ The sad story **tugged at our heartstrings**
tremendously.

同義：動人肺腑　Come home to one's heart.

yǒu yí lì bì yǒu yí bì

有一利必有一弊

Nothing is perfect.

If you would enjoy the fire, you must put up with the
  smoke.

There is no fire without some smoke.

No rose without a thorn.

 A decent boldness does not help although it
  expresses your view, **nothing is perfect**.

yǒu mù gòng dǔ

有目共睹

It is for all the world to see.

As clear as daylight.

One would be blind not to see.

Dazzling to the eye.

Stick out a mile.

There is a witness everywhere.

 It is for all the world to see that John is an honest
  gentleman.

yǒu míng wú shí
有名無實
A rope of sand.

In name but not in deed.
In name only.

 The new title does not mean that he is promoted, it's but **a rope of sand**.

 國語 · 晉語：〝宣子曰，吾有卿之名而無其實。〞

> **同義：**徒有虛名
> What good can it do an ass to be called a lion?

> **反義：**名不虛傳　Worthy of the name.

六畫

yǒu zhì shì jìng chéng
有志事竟成
Where there's a will there's a way.

It's dogged that does it.
A wilful man will have his way.

Through his industry John won the scholarship, **where there's a will there's a way**.

 後漢書 · 耿弇傳："有志者事竟成也。"

同義：世上無難事，只怕有心人

Nothing is impossible to a willing heart.

反義：謀事在人，成事在天

Man proposes, God disposes.

---

yǒu tiáo bù wěn
有條不紊
In trim.

In apple-pie order.
Keep ship-shape.

 The boat was put **in trim** for sailing.

 尚書 · 盤庚上："若網在綱，有條不紊。"

反義：亂七八糟　At sixes and sevens.

---

yǒu bèi wú huàn

有備無患

Have a second string to one's bow.

Though the sun shines, leave not your cloak at home.
Forewarned is forearmed.

 To **have a second string to his bow**, Tom always
has two plans for one project.

 左傳·襄十一年："居安思危，思則有備，有備無
患。"

yǒu guò zhī ér wú bù jí

有過之而無不及

Go too far.

To err on the safe side.
Do a thing to a fault.
By a long chalk.
Overshoot the mark.

 You **went too far** by giving so much money to
that beggar.

六
畫

成語故事：To err is human

通常譯作"人孰無過"，原來是拉丁古訓 Humanum est errare 的英譯，於十六世紀期間傳入英國。詩人 Alexander Pope（1688-1744）的詩中曾有：To err is human, to forgive divine 之句，傳誦一時，成為名句，因此有人以為此語是他的創作，認為此句典於詩人之作中。泰晤時報文學副刊曾評此句說：現代道德研究家（moralist）對甚麼都加以原諒，因為他們除了「人孰無過」外對任何其他事物都不能肯定。

yǒu fú tóng xiǎng yǒu huò tóng dāng

有福同享，有禍同當

For better or for worse.

Friendships multiply joys and divide griefs.
Throw in one's lot with

 Let us face the trouble together, **for better or for worth**.

> **同義**：休戚與共　In weal or woe.

> **反義**：有酒有肉多兄弟，急難何曾見一人
> In time of prosperity friends will be plenty; in
> time of adversity not one among twenty.

hàn liú jiá bèi
汗流浹背
All of a muck of sweat.

Drenched with sweat.
In a sweat.
Perspire profusely.

 We have to carry out such a major project with **all of a muck of sweat**.

 後漢書‧伏皇后紀：“操去，顧左右，汗流浹背。”

jiāng shān yì gǎi běn xìng nán yí
江山易改，本性難移
What is bred in the bone will never come out of the flesh.

You cannot make a crab walk straight.

The child is father to the man.
The fox changes his skin but not his habits.
The leopard can't change its spots.

例句 Corrupted officials, as **what is bred in the bone (will never come out of the flesh)**, are looking for bribes.

同義：萬變不離其宗
　　　Once a knave and always a knave.

成語故事：The leopard does not change his spots

　　此語以豹不會改變皮上的斑點喻一個人的本性難改。通常認為這是典於聖經舊約耶利米書第十三章第二十三節。（古實人豈能改變皮膚呢。豹豈能改變斑點呢。）

本性難改見於生活習慣，因此這句話也常用以指一個人的習慣不易改變，倒如史考特（J. Scott）在 Clutch of Vipers 形容一個老頭子：He always was a dirty old man...and the leopard doesn't change his spots.（他從來就是個糟老頭子……江山易改，本性難易。）

jiāng hé rì xià

江河日下

Go from bad to worse.

Go down drain.

Get worse and worse.

 Programs of the television are **going from bad to worse**.

王士禎：「至於漢魏樂府古選之遺音，蕩然無復存者，江河日下，滔滔不及。」

同義：每況愈下　Out of the frying pan into the fire.
反義：蒸蒸日上　Grow with each passing day.

jiāng láng cái jìn

江郎才盡

At the end of one's tether.

At one's wit's end.

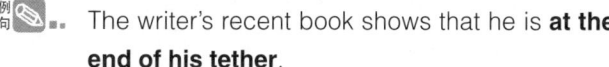 The writer's recent book shows that he is **at the end of his tether**.

六畫

> **同義**：智窮才盡　At the end of one's rope.
>
> **反義**：滿腹妙計　To be full of wrinkles.

huī xīn sàng zhì
灰心喪志
In the dumps.

In black despair.
To lose heart.

 George is (down) **in the dumps** because he lost his pay envelope.

> **同義**：意氣消沉　Have one's heart in one's boots.
>
> **反義**：發奮有為　Shake oneself together.

bǎi chuān guī hǎi
百川歸海
Follow the river and you'll get to the sea.

The sea refuses no river.
All rivers do what they can for the sea.
All roads lead to Rome.

例句 ▪ To find the cause is easy as you **follow the river and you'll get to the sea**.

出處 ▪ 淮南子‧氾論訓：「百川異源，而皆歸於海。」

> **同義**：異途同歸
> There are more ways to the wood than one.

bǎi chǐ gān tóu gèng jìn yí bù
百尺竿頭，更進一步
Make further efforts.

Break one's own record.

例句 ▪ You have to **make further efforts** to do a better job.

出處 ▪ 傳燈錄：「百尺竿頭須進步，十方世界是全身。」

> **同義**：精益求精
> Though good is good, yet better is better.
>
> **反義**：吃老本　Rest on one's laurels.

六畫

bǎi zhé bù náo

百折不撓

Fight for it tooth and nail.

Get at it hammer and tongs.
Never say die.
Stick it out.

例句 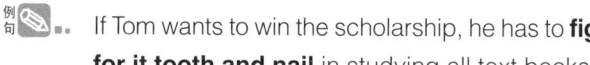 If Tom wants to win the scholarship, he has to **fight for it tooth and nail** in studying all text books.

出處 漢 · 蔡邕：「有百折不撓，臨大節而不可奪之風。」

> **同義：**不屈不撓　Firm and unyielding.

> **反義：**俯首就範　Give one's head for the washing.

bǎi wú liáo lài

百無聊賴

It's more pain to do nothing than something.

Have time hanging on one's hands.
Bored stiff.

例句 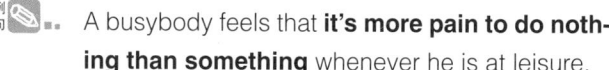 A busybody feels that **it's more pain to do nothing than something** whenever he is at leisure.

同義：閒極無聊　Twiddle one's thumbs.

反義：忙不過來　Have too many irons in the fire.

bǎi wén bù rú yí jiàn
百聞不如一見

Seeing is believing.

One eye-witness is better than ten ear-witnesses.

例句　We visited the West Lake. **Seeing is believing**, it is really beautiful.

同義：耳聞不如目睹
The eyes believe themselves, the ears believe other people.

六
畫

lǎo shēng cháng tán
老生常談

Standing dish.

A tale twice told is cabbage twice sold.
Flog a dead horse.

There is nothing new in his speech, just a **standing dish**.

 三國志 · 魏志 · 管輅傳："此老生之常譚。"

> **反義**：奇談怪論　A cock and bull story.

lǎo chéng liàn dá
老成練達
Know one's way about.

To have cut one's eyeteeth.
Know one's onions (stuff).

 He **knows his way about** and should be able to handle the case.

> **同義**：久經世故　Have seen the elephant.

> **反義**：乳臭未乾　One's mouth is full of pap.

lǎo mǎ shí tú
老馬識途
An old dog for a hard road.

One who has been around.

An old ox makes a straight furrow.

If you wish for good advice, consult an old man.

They who live longest will see most.

例句 **As an old dog for a hard road**, Tom gets on with his new work very well.

出處 韓非子‧説林上：“乃放老馬而隨之，遂得道。”

> **同義：**駕輕就熟　An old hand at the game.

lǎo dāng yì zhuàng
老當益壯

Live to a green old age.

To be hale and hearty.

There is fight in the old dog yet.

例句 The artist, **living to a green old age**, painted the mural when he was eighty.

出處 後漢書‧馬援傳：“丈夫為志，窮當益堅，老當益壯。”

> **同義：**人老心不老，人窮志不窮
> Life begins at sixty.

ěr rú mù rǎn
耳濡目染

He that keeps company with the wolf will learn to howl.

Under the influence of

例句 ■ The boy takes to the game machine, **he that keeps company with the wolf will learn to howl**.

出處 ■ 昌黎先生集・清河郡公房公墓碣銘："目濡耳染，不學以能。"

> **反義**：出污泥而不染
> Lilies are whitest in a blackamoor's hand.

zì lì gēng shēng
自力更生

Stand on one's own feet.

Pull oneself up by the footstraps.

例句 ■ He **stands on his own feet** to start his own business.

> **同義**：發憤圖強　Shake oneself together.

> **反義**：寄人籬下　To eat out of one's hand.

zì yǐ wéi shì

自以為是

Too sure of oneself.

Self-opinionated.

例句 ▪▪ Don't be **too sure of yourself** about what you want to say in the meeting.

出處 ▪▪ 荀子・榮辱："凡鬥者必自以為是，而以人為非也。"

同義：剛愎自用　Reckon without one's host.
反義：不恥下問　Bow down thy ear.

zì yóu zì zài

自由自在

In a state of bliss.

As free as (the) air.
As free as a bird.

例句 ▪▪ Tom felt **in a state of bliss** when he was left alone to do the job.

出處 ▪▪ 景德傳燈錄："問牛頭未見四祖時如何，師日，自由自在，問先後如何，師日，自由自在。"

同義：舒舒服服　As snug as a bug in a rug.

反義：侷促不安　To be ill at ease.

zì zuò zì shòu
自作自受
Suffer for what one does.

One must drink as one brews.
He that handles thorns shall prick his fingers.
As you make your bed, so you must lie on it.
Fry in one's own grease.
Serve one right.

例句 ■■ He did not listen to me and **suffers for what he has done**.

出處 ■■ 釋普濟．五燈會元："僧問金山穎，一百二十斤鐵枷，教阿誰擔，穎曰，自作自受。"

同義：作繭自縛　Caught in one's own trap.

zì gào fèn yǒng

自告奮勇

To bell the cat.

Take upon oneself.
Accept the challenge.
Bravely offer.

 John volunteered **to bell the cat** to ask the president for bonus to all workers.

zì wǒ táo zuì

自我陶醉

Each bird loves to hear himself sing.

As the fool thinks, so the bell chinks.
Congratulate oneself on
In one's glory.
Licks one's chops.

 He plays violin poorly every evening; **each bird loves to hear himself sing**.

六
畫

zì mìng bù fán

自命不凡

Think one is the whole cheese.

Think something of oneself.
To be full of oneself.
Pique oneself on
Everyone can keep house better than her mother, till she tries.

 She sings well but **thinks** that **she is the whole cheese** and refuses to join our chorus.

同義：自命清高　Holier-than-thou
反義：妄自菲薄　Make oneself too cheap.

zì shí qí lì

自食其力

Earn one's own bread.

Shift for oneself.
Cut one's own grass.
Paddle one's own canoe.
Hoe one's own row.

例句 ▪▪ With no one to look after her, the old woman sells newspapers to **earn her own bread**.

出處 ▪▪ 太平經："各自衣食其力。"

> **反義：**借債度日　Live on ticket.

成語故事：Catch not at the shadow and lose the substance

此語直譯作"不要捕影而失去本物"。伊索寓言中有一則寫一隻狗叼着肉骨過橋時見到水中另有一隻狗口中叼着肉骨。此狗貪心想去搶那狗的肉骨，張口要吠，結果口叼的本物肉骨掉落水中。寓言的教訓就是：Catch not at the shadow and lose the substance，捕風捉影，一無所得，反而失去了實在的東西。這個成語據說流行於十六世紀中期，一說是一句古老的俗諺；但一般認為它像許多格言一樣出於伊索寓言。

六畫

zì shí qí guǒ

自食其果

Stew in one's own juice.

As you brew, so you must drink.
Fry in one's own grease.

 I warned him that if he didn't follow the rules he
would **stew in his own juice**.

> **同義**：自作自受
>
> As you make your bed, so you must lie on it.

zì qiáng bù xī

自強不息

Shake oneself together.

Brace up.
Stand on one's feet.
Work one's way up.
Buck one's ideas up.

 One has to **shake oneself together** to earn a good
position.

出處 周易・乾："天行健，君子以自強不息。"

同義：奮發有為	Rouse oneself to action.
反義：自暴自棄	Abandon oneself to despair.

zì dé qí lè
自得其樂
Take delight in

He is happy that thinks himself so.
Get a kick out of
The world is his that enjoys it.

例句 ■■ John has a poor voice, but he **takes delight in** singing.

出處 ■■ 明‧陶宗儀‧輟耕錄：「雌雄和鳴，自得其樂。」

反義：自尋煩惱　To fret one's gizzard.

zì qī qī rén
自欺欺人
The magician mutters, and knows not what he mutters.

Liars begin by imposing upon others, but end by deceiving themselves.

六
畫

例句 He has no money in his account but writes checks to pay debts, **magician mutters and not knows what he mutters**.

出處 大學："所謂誠其意者,毋自欺也。"

zì míng dé yì
自鳴得意
Like a dog with two tails.

Cry roast meat.
Pat oneself on the back.
To crow over
To be corned with oneself.
Preen oneself.

例句 Tom bragged about his gain **like a dog with two tails**.

> **反義**:大喊倒霉　Get it in the neck.

zì bào zì qì
自暴自棄
Ruin oneself.

Abandon oneself to despair.

Cut one's own throat.
Stand in one's own light.

例句 ■■ To indulge in drinking is to **ruin oneself**.

出處 ■■ 孟子・離婁上："自暴者，不可與有言也。自棄者，
不可與有為也。"

> **反義**：發憤圖強　Shake oneself together.

xuè qì fāng gāng
血氣方剛
Full of vim and vigour.

In one's raw youth.
In the prime of youth.
To be in the green.
In one's salad days.

例句 ■■ Man at twenty is **full of vim and vigour**.

出處 ■■ 論語・季氏："及其壯也，血氣方剛，戒之在鬥。"

> **反義**：老氣橫秋　To be stricken in years.

háng háng chū zhuàng yuán

行行出狀元

Every one can reach the top of the ladder.

There are many ways to fame.
In every art it is good to have a master.

 Working hard and with determination, **everyone can reach the top of the ladder** in one's trade.

xíng jiāng jiù mù

行將就木

Have one foot in the grave.

On one's last legs.
At death's door.
The old man's staff is a knocker at death's door.

 She is almost ninety, **having one foot in the grave** already.

 左傳·僖二十三年："公子重耳謂季隗曰，待我二十五年不來而後嫁。季隗曰：我二十五年矣，又如是而嫁，則就木焉，請待子。"

同義：日薄西山　Sinking fast.
反義：方興未艾　In the bud.

yī guān chǔ chǔ

衣冠楚楚

Well groomed.

Dressed up to the ninety nines.
To dress within an inch of one's life.
In full feather (fig).

例句 ■■ A **well groomed** gentleman is welcomed everywhere.

出處 ■■ 詩經 · 曹風 · 蜉蝣： "衣裳楚楚。"

同義：盛裝冠戴　In full fig.
反義：衣衫襤褸　To be out at elbows.

yī shān lán lǚ

衣衫襤褸

Out at elbows.

Down at the heels.

例句 ■■ The beggar is **out at elbows** in the market.

同義：鶉衣百結　To be threadbare.

hé zú guà chǐ
何足掛齒
Don't mention it.

Nothing to speak of.

例句 ■ It's a little token. **Don't mention it**.

出處 ■ 史記: "何足掛牙齒間。"

同義:不值一提　Nothing to make a song about.
反義:膾炙人口　To be in everyone's mouth.

zuò wēi zuò fú
作威作福
Lord it over.

Throw one's weight about.
Push people around.

例句 ■ The husband **lorded it over** his household.

出處 ■ 尚書 · 洪範: "惟辟作福,惟辟作威。……臣無有作福作威。"

同義:專橫跋扈　Play the bully.
反義:畢恭畢敬　Cap in hand.

zuò zéi xīn xū

作賊心虛

Have a guilty conscience.

He that lives ill, fear follows him.
He that commits a fault thinks eveyone speaks of it.
A bully is always a coward.

 The officer **has a guilty conscience** for having accept "gifts".

 宋・悟明・聯燈會要："卻顧侍者云，適來有人看方丈麼，侍者云有，師云，作賊人心虛。"

> **反義：**平生不作虧心事，半夜敲門也不驚
> A quiet conscience sleeps in thunder.

zuò jiǎn zì fù

作繭自縛

Sow the wind and reap the whirlwind.

Caught in one's own trap.
Fry in one's own grease.
Hoist with one's own petard.

 He has put his entire fortune on the venture, **sowing the wind and reaping the whirlwind**.

七
畫

出處 ■ 傳燈錄："志公坐禪，如蠶吐絲自縛。"

| **同義**：自作自受 | One must drink as one brews. |
| **反義**：衝破藩籬 | To break bounds. |

kè jǐ fèng gōng
克己奉公
Do one's bit.

Keep up one's end.

例句 ■ In a prosperous society, every one **does one's bit**.

出處 ■ 後漢書・祭遵傳："遵為人廉約小心，克己奉公。"

| **同義**：盡忠職守 | Fulfil one's trust. |
| **反義**：尸位素餐 | Feast at the public crib. |

kè qín kè jiǎn
克勤克儉
Industry is fortune's right hand, and frugality her left.

例句 ■ Tom succeeded because he worked hard and **industry is fortune's right hand, and frugality her left**.

出處 ■■ 尚書・大禹謨：「克勤於邦，克儉於家。」

> **反義：**好吃懶做　Eat one's head off.

lěng ruò bīng shuāng
冷若冰霜

As cold as charity (ice).

An iceberg.

例句 ■■ She treated her ex-husband **as cold as charity**.

> **同義：**給以冷遇　Give one the cold shoulder.

> **反義：**熱情洋溢　Glow with enthusiasm.

lěng yǎn páng guān
冷眼旁觀

To be outside the ropes.

Treat with indifference.

例句 ■■ Let us **be outside the ropes** to see which way the wind blows.

出處 ■■ 元曲：「常將冷眼觀螃蟹，看你橫行到幾時。」

七畫

同義：袖手旁觀	Look on with folded arms.
反義：熱烈贊助	Carry a torch for

bié yǒu yòng xīn
別有用心
Have an axe to grind.

With an ulterior purpose.
Have an end in view.
Have something up one's sleeve.

 The world is full of people with **axes to grind**. So, be careful.

> **反義**：心地光明
> Have one's heart in the right place.

lì lìng zhì hūn
利令智昏
Wealth makes wit waver.

Greedy for money.

 He has put his fortune on shares as **wealth makes wit waver**.

出處 ■ 史記‧平原君虞卿列傳：“鄙諺曰，利令智昏。”

成語故事：Every man has his price

直譯作"人各有價"，是有譏刺意義的諺語，以其意指任何人都可以用錢收買。此語經英國政治家華爾浦爾（Robert Walpole，1676-1745，英國第一任首相）說的：All those men have their price。（那些人都有他們的價錢）而被視為是他創始的名句。但是事實上在他之前已經作為古諺有人用過。同時這種想法也早見於古希臘哲學家伊壁鳩魯（Epictetus，公元前341-270）的著作中，原是一句古諺。

pǐ jí tài lái
否極泰來

When things are at the worst, they will mend.

They that sow in tears shall reap in joy.
The darkest hour is that before the dawn.

例句 ■ Do not cry over the spilt milk, **when things are at the worst, they will mend**.

出處 ■ 白居易 · 遣懷詩: "樂往必悲生,泰來猶否極。"

同義:苦盡甘來　Pain past is pleasure.

反義:興盡悲來
He who laughs on Friday will weep on
Sunday.

chuī máo qiú cī
吹毛求疵
Split hairs.

Pick a hole in one's coat.
Pick to pieces.
Find fault with.
Number the streaks of the tulip.

例句 ■ The boss is **splitting hairs** to find faults with us.

出處 ■ 韓非子 · 大體: "不吹毛而求小疵,不洗垢而察難
知。"

hán hú qí cí
含糊其詞
To be soft-spoken.

Hum and ha.

Beat about the bush.

例句 He **is soft-spoken** in explaining why he did so.

同義：支吾其詞
Speak with one's tongue in one's cheek.

反義：毫不含糊 Make no bones of

hú lún tūn zǎo
囫圇吞棗
To bone up.

To learn by rote.

例句 Mr. Wong is **boning up** on English for the test.

出處 朱子語錄："道是個有條理的，不是囫圇底物。"

同義：生吞活剝 Copy blindly.

反義：細味品嘗 Enjoy the full gusto of

七
畫

zuò lì bù ān
坐立不安
Give one the fidgets.

Sit on a bag of fleas.
Have ants in one's pants.

例句 The news about the accident **gives everyone the fidgets**.

同義：忐忑不安　In a fidget.
反義：高枕無憂　A good conscience is a soft pillow.

zuò yán qǐ xíng
坐言起行
Say well is good, but do well is better.

例句 You have to fulfil your promise as to **say well is good, but to do well is better**.

出處 荀子・性惡："故坐而之，起而可設，張而可施行。"

同義：說到做到　Live up to one's words.
反義：誇誇其談 The greatest talkers are always the least doers.

zuò xiǎng qí chéng

坐享其成

One beat the bush and another caught the hare.

Get something for nothing.
Unearned income.

例句 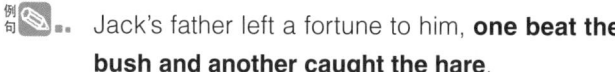 Jack's father left a fortune to him, **one beat the bush and another caught the hare**.

出處 孟子：＂千歲之日至，可坐而致也。＂

同義：衣來伸手，飯來張口
Kitty Swerrock where she sat, come reach me this, come reach me that.

反義：為人作嫁　Be in attendance on

---

zuò shí shān kōng

坐食山空

Dig one's grave with one's teeth.

Eat out of house and home.
Always taking out of a meal-tub, and never putting
in, soon comes to the bottom.

例句 The man is too lazy to do anything, **digging his grave with his teeth**.

七畫

京本通俗小説 · 錯斬崔寧：〝坐吃山空，立吃地陷。〞

> **反義**：勤儉起家
> Industry is fortune's right hand and frugality her left.

zī zī bú juàn

孜孜不倦

With tireless energy.

To peg away.
Grind away at
Knuckle down to it.
Keep the cart on the wheels.
Keep one's nose to the grindstone.
Knock oneself out.

 Lily practiced **with tireless energy** for the coming piano contest.

 後漢書 · 魯丕傳：〝丕性沈深好學，孳孳不倦。〞

> **同義**：埋頭苦幹　Work like a Trojan.

> **反義**：游手好閒　Fool away one's time.

nòng qiǎo chéng zhuō

弄巧成拙

Ride one's horse to death.

Make a mess of things.

例句 ▪▪ To boast about one's past is to **ride one's horse to death**.

出處 ▪▪ 黃庭堅・拙軒頌：“弄巧成拙，為蛇添足。”

同義：機關算盡太聰明　To lose one's reckoning

xíng dān yǐng zhī

形單影隻

All alone.

His hat covers his family.
A confirmed bachelor.
An old maid.
All by oneself.

例句 ▪▪ He is **all alone** in the party.

出處 ▪▪ 韓愈・祭十二郎文：“兩世一身，形單影隻。”

同義：孤雲野鶴　Keep oneself to oneself.

反義：魚貫而出　In Indian file.

七畫

rěn qì tūn shēng
忍氣吞聲
Swallow the leek.

Swallow one's pride.
Eat dirt.
As patient as Job.

 You don't have to **swallow the leek** if it is not your fault.

同義：捺着性子　Bottle up one's feelings.
反義：大發雷霆　Explode with rage.

rěn rǔ fù zhòng
忍辱負重
As patient as an ox.

Stoop to conquer.
Pocket an insult.
Eat boiled crow.
Bear with evil, and expect good.

 He waited **as patient as an ox** for a chance to clear his name.

三國志・吳志・陸遜傳：「國家所以屈諸君使相承望者，以僕有尺寸可稱，能忍辱負重故也。」

同義：臥薪嘗膽　To nurse vengeance.

rěn wú kě rěn
忍無可忍
Beyond one's endurance.

Patience runs out.
Even a worm will turn.
The last straw breaks the camel's back.

 He fought back because the insult was **beyond his endurance**.

同義：是可忍孰不可忍
　　　More than flesh and blood can bear.

反義：百忍成金
　　　All good things come to those who wait.

七畫

kuài dāo zhǎn luàn má

快刀斬亂麻

Take drastic measures.

Cut the Gordian knot.
Get it over and done with.

 The King, **taking drastic measures**, ordered his
army to burn down the village.

同義：乾脆利落　To be clear-cut.	
反義：優柔寡斷　To be neither off nor on.	

wǒ xíng wǒ sù

我行我素

To be a law unto oneself.

Take one's own course.
Go one's own way.
Call one's soul one's own.

 He paid no heed to your advice, **to be a law unto
himself**, gave a rude answer to the director.

fú wēi jì kùn

扶危濟困

Be a good Samaritan.

Help a lame dog over a stile.

例句 ▪ **Be a good Samaritan** and contribute much to the fund.

出處 ▪ 水滸記傳奇：〝宋公明他扶危濟困隱功曹。〞

同義：見義勇為　Do a good turn.

反義：落井下石
When a dog is drowing, everyone offers him a drink.

成語故事：Be a good Samaritan

英語以 Samaritan 指〝樂善好施〞。樂善好施的人稱為 a good samaritan。貧民救濟基金稱為 a Samaritan Fund，以此詞作形容詞。此詞暗示源於聖經新約路加福音中提到的撒瑪利亞人。此人見到一個被強盜搶劫、毒打、剝光衣服躺在地上沒人理會的人，扶救照應他，非常周到。（見路加福音第十章第三十三至三十七節。）1953 年在倫敦成立救濟機構以 Samaritans 為名。現有不少義務工作人員，分會遍佈全球。

七畫

fú yáo zhí shàng
扶搖直上
On the upgrade.

Step by step the ladder is ascended.
On the up and up.

例句 Business of the shop is **on the upgrade**.

出處 莊子 · 逍遙遊："搏扶搖羊角而上者九萬里。"

同義：蒸蒸日上　Grow with each passing day.
反義：每況愈下　Out of the flying pan into the fire.

tóu qí suǒ hào
投其所好
Suit one's fancy.

Scratch a person where he itches.
A drop of honey catches more flies than a hogshead
　　of vinegar.

例句 Jack bought Jean a scarf to **suit her fancy**.

同義：拍馬屁　Butter someone up.
反義：拂逆人意　Rub one up the wrong way.

gǎi xié guī zhèng

改邪歸正

To mend one's way.

 The thief **mended his way** and worked as a hawker.

同義：去惡從善　Eschew evil, and do good.
反義：誤入歧途　To have gone astray.

gǎi tóu huàn miàn

改頭換面

A new deal.

A changed version.

 It's **a new deal** for a thief to work as a hawker.

 古今風謠：〝漢似胡兒胡似漢，改頭換面總一般。〞

同義：裝點門面　Put up a front.
反義：原封不動　To be left intact.

七

畫

gōng qí bú bèi

攻其不備

Take one napping

Take one off his guard.
To catch a weasel asleep.

例句 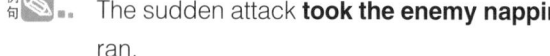 The sudden attack **took the enemy napping** and ran.

出處 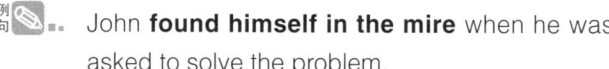 孫子 · 計篇: "攻其不備,出其不意。"

同義:突然襲擊　Swoop down upon
反義:鳴鼓而攻之　Beat a charge.

shù shǒu wú cè

束手無策

Find oneself in the mire.

At a loss what to do.
Throw up one's hands in despair.
Not know which way to turn (jump).

例句 John **found himself in the mire** when he was asked to solve the problem.

出處 宋季三朝政要：「檜（秦檜）死而逆亮（金主完顏亮）南牧，孰不束手無策。」

同義：一籌莫展　To be at one's wit's end.
反義：滿腹妙計　To be full of wrinkles.

qǐ rén yōu tiān
杞人憂天
Meet trouble halfway.

Borrow trouble.

例句 What's the use for us to **meet this trouble halfway**.

出處 列子・天瑞：「杞國有人，憂天崩墜，身無所寄。」

同義：無病呻吟　Cry out before one is hurt.
反義：泰山崩於前而目不瞬 　　　If the sky falls we shall catch larks.

七畫

bù rén hòu chén
步人後塵
Tread in one's footsteps.

Follow upon one's heels.

Take a leaf out of another's book.
Follow the beaten track.

 Harold **treads on his father's footsteps** to become a lawyer.

同義：蕭規曹隨　Go on in the same old rut.
反義：別開生面　Break fresh ground.

mě kuàng yù xià
每況愈下
Go down drain.

Go from bad to worse.
Out of the parlour into the kitchen.
Out of the frying-pan into the fire.
To be on the wane.

 Look at the record and you see our business has **gone down drain**.

同義：一蟹不如一蟹　From a smoke into smother.
反義：蒸蒸日上　Grow with each passing day.

chén mò guǎ yán

沉默寡言

Hold one's peace (tongue).

To be a regular oyster.
A person of few words.

 He is used to **hold his peace** in meetings.

同義：默不作聲　Refrain from comment.
反義：滔滔不絕　Talk oneself out of breath.

jiàn lì wàng yì

見利忘義

Double cross one for money.

Honour and profit lie not in one sack.
Two dogs over one bone seldom agree.

 That guy will do everything to **double cross one for money**.

 漢書："夫賣友者，謂見利而忘義也。"

七畫

jiàn yì sī qiān
見異思遷

Grass is always greener on the other side of the fence (hill).

A rolling stone.

 Jack has been to Tom's office, feeling that **grass is always greener on the other side of the fence** and so decided to find a new job.

 國語 · 齊語："少而習焉,其心安焉,不見異物而思遷焉。"

> **反義**：固步自封
> He that stays in the valley shall never get over the hill.

jiàn yì yǒng wéi
見義勇為

Help a lame dog over a stile.

Do a good turn.
Be a good Samaritan.
Take heart of grace to

例句 ■ ■ John ran after the thief to get the purse back to the woman in the so-called **helping a lame dog over a stile** action.

出處 ■ ■ 論語 · 為政：「見義不為，是無勇也。」

> **反義**：見死不救　Leave one in the lurch.

yán zhī wú wù
言之無物
Hollow words.

Empty talk.
A deluge of words and a drop of sense.

例句 ■ ■ The politician's speech is nothing but **hollow words**.

> **反義**：話中有話　There's a catch in one's words.

yán xíng yí zhì
言行一致
Suit the action to the word.

Practise what you preach.
As good as one's word.

Mean what one says.

 To **suit the action to the word**, he contributed a lot of money to the fund as he promised.

> **同義**：坐言起行
> Say well is good, but do well is better.

> **反義**：説一套做一套
> Say one thing and do another.

yán yóu zài ěr
言猶在耳
Fresh in one's mind.

Still ring in one's ears.

 Your promise is still **fresh in my mind** and now you refuse to pay my money back.

 左傳 · 文七年："今君雖終，言猶在耳。"

> **反義**：左耳入，右耳出
> In at one ear and out at the other.

yán guò qí shí

言過其實

To make a mountain out of a mole hill.

Overshoot oneself (the mark).
Draw the long bow.
Stretch the truth.
Paint the devil blacker than he is.
The lion is not so fierce as he is painted.

 He is **making a mountain out of mole hill** when he said that he lost all his belongings.

 三國志 · 馬良傳：" 馬謖言過其實，不能大用。"

同義：過甚其詞
　　　　The devil is not so black as he is painted.

反義：輕描淡寫　To skate over

---

yán jiǎn yì gāi

言簡意賅

Precise and to the point.

Brevity is the soul of wit.
Speak little and to the purpose.
To hit it off.

七
畫

To be sparing of words.
Short and sweet.

 John's advice is **precise and to the point**.

> **反義**：叨叨嘮嘮　To chew the rag.

zǒu tóu wú lù
走投無路
In a tight spot.

Stand at bay.
To be driven to the wall.

 He was **in a tight spot** when the bank asked him to pay the loan.

 元曲選・楊顯之・瀟湘雨："淋的我走投無路。"

> **同義**：到處碰壁　Driven from pillar to post.

> **反義**：左右逢源
> It is good to have friends both in heaven and in hell.

zǒu mǎ kàn huā

走馬看花

Hit the high spots.

Go sight-seeing.
A brief fleeting look.

例句 ■■ We spent a week in China **hitting the high spots**.

出處 ■■ 孟郊詩：〝春風得意馬蹄疾，一日看遍長安花。〞

> **反義**：流連忘返　Can't tear oneself away.

zú zhì duō móu

足智多謀

Fruitful of expedients.

Have plenty of brains.

例句 ■■ The way he deals with the case proves that he is **fruitful of expedients**.

出處 ■■ 元曲選 · 連環計：〝此人足智多謀，可與共事。〞

> **同義**：精明強幹　To be up to snuff.

> **反義**：愚不可及　No fool like an old fool.

七畫

shēn bài míng liè
身敗名裂
Shorn of one's glory.

Die like a dog.
Fall into disgrace.
To be under a cloud.
Come down in the world.

 The scandal left him **shorn of his glory**.

 辛稼軒 · 賀新郎詞："將軍百戰身名裂。"

> **反義**：名噪一時　To rise to fame.

---

shēn tǐ lì xíng
身體力行
Practise what one preaches.

Put into practice.

 An honest man **practices what he preaches**.

 淮南子 · 氾論訓："故聖人以身體之。" / 禮記 · 中庸："力行近乎仁。"

同義：以身作則	Set a good example for others.
反義：言行不一	Say one thing and do another.

xùn léi bù jí yǎn ěr

迅雷不及掩耳

It came absolutely out of the blue.

As swift as lightning.
Before you could say Jack Robinson.

例句　**It came absolutely out of the blue** when John asked Lily to marry him during the tea time.

出處　六韜·軍勢："疾雷不及掩耳，迅電不及暝目。"

反義：慢條斯理	As slow as molasses in winter.

fáng huàn wèi rán

防患未然

Prevention is better than cure.

Nip in the bud.
Crush in the egg.
To take precaution.

七畫

例句 ■■ Thievery is common in this area. Better lock the door as **prevention is better than cure**.

出處 ■■ 漢書・外戚傳："事不當固爭，防禍於未然。"

> **同義**：杜漸防微　A little fire is quickly trodden out.

> **反義**：賊去關門
>
> Lock the stable door after the horse is stolen.

成語故事：He sets the fox to keep the geese

　　安排狐狸去保護鵝，喻信賴不可信的人，我們説的"所託非人"也。伊索寓言中關於狐狸的故事很多，而以 a fox in a lamb's skin，披羊皮的狐狸喻偽君子（亦作 a wolf in sheep's clothing），更是常用之詞。聖經新約馬太福音第七章第十五節有：Beware of false prophets, which come to you in sheep's clothing, but inwardly they are ravening wolves。（你們要防備假先知。他們到你們這裏來，外面披着羊皮，裏面卻是殘暴的狼。）不可不防！

tǎn tè bù ān

忐忑不安

Get hot under the collar.

In a fidget.
To be high-strung.
To be on nettles.
Like a hen on a hot griddle.

 No need to **get hot under collar** for such a small mistake.

同義：心緒不寧	Get out of bed on the wrong side.
反義：泰然自若	At one's ease.

bìng jià qí qū

並駕齊驅

Keep abreast (pace) with

Shoulder to shoulder.

 Keep abreast with progress and you'll be promoted.

 劉勰·文心雕龍：「並駕齊驅，而一轂統輻。」

八畫

同義：齊頭並進	Neck and Neck
反義：遙遙領先	Streets ahead of

shì bù yí chí
事不宜遲
There's no time to lose.

It brooks no delay.
The matter asks haste.
Not let the grass grow under one's feet.
Delays are dangerous.

例句 ■■ Action now for **there's no time to lose**.

同義：勿失時機	Now or never.
反義：勿操之過急	
	Draw not thy bow before thy arrow be fixed.

shì zài rén wéi
事在人為
Fortune favours the brave.

Where there's a will there's a way.

It's dogged that does it.

 Do not wait for luck as **fortune favours the brave**.

同義：有志事竟成　A wilful man will have his way.

反義：人算不如天算 An ounce of luck is better than a pound of wisdom.

shì bèi gōng bàn
事倍功半
For all one's efforts.

Be a fool for one's pains.
Make bricks without straw.

 Hard working will pay **for all one's efforts**.

 語本《孟子‧公孫丑上》

同義：吃力不討好　Bite on granite.

八畫

yī yī bù shě
依依不捨
Leave one with regret.

Can't tear oneself away.

例句 ■■ The boy **left his mother with regret**.

出處 ■■ 楚辭： "戀戀兮依依。"

> **反義**：避之則吉　Steer clear of

gōng bù yìng qiú
供不應求
Supply short of demand.

Demand over supply.

例句 ■■ The **supply of meat is short of demand** as New Year Festival is near at hand.

> **同義**：僧多粥少　Not enough to go round.

> **反義**：取之無禁，用之不竭
> The more the well is used, the more water it gives.

lái rì fāng cháng

來日方長

No need to hurry.

There's plenty of time yet.

It can wait.

One of these days.

One of these days is none of these days.

Tomorrow is another day.

A day to come shows longer than a year that's gone.

 Never say it's **no need to hurry** in doing anything because time flies.

 朱子語錄："勿謂今日不學而有來日。"

> **反義：急不及待　To be bursting to do something.**

liǎng bài jù shāng

兩敗俱傷

Both suffer for it.

Fight like Kilkenny cats.

Quarrelling dogs come halting home.

 They fought in the boxing for the champion cup so fiercely that **both suffered for it**.

八畫

出處 ■■ 戰國策："今兩虎爭人而鬥，小者必死，大者必傷。"

qí mào bù yáng
其貌不揚

As ugly as a scarecrow.

例句 ■■ He was not accepted because he looks **as ugly as a scarecrow**.

出處 ■■ 全唐文・裴度・自題寫真贊："爾才不長，爾貌不揚。"

同義：獐頭鼠目　With a hangdog look.
反義：一表人才　Manners make the man.

kè bù róng huǎn
刻不容緩

Call for immediate attention.

Not a moment to lose.
Brook no delay.

例句 ■■ The urgent case **calls for our immediate attention**.

同義：	事不宜遲	The matter asks haste.
反義：	來日方長	There's plenty of time yet.

qǔ ér dài zhī
取而代之
Elbow out someone.

Step into a person's shoes.
Fill a person's bonnet (shoes).
Put a person's nose out of joint.
Take the place of
Edge out someone.

 Tom did not apply for the position as he does not like to **elbow out someone** for it.

 史記・項羽本紀： "籍曰，彼可取而代之。"

duō duō bī rén
咄咄逼人
Play the bully.

Lord it over.
To be overbearing.

八
畫

It is the coward that always **play the bully**.

 法書要錄："王濛子修，善隸行，子敬每者修書云，咄咄逼人。"

同義：盛氣凌人　Throw one's weight about.
反義：溫柔敦厚　As harmless as a dove.

hū zhī jí lái huī zhī jí qù
呼之即來，揮之即去
At one's beck and call.

 The boss has many workers **at his beck and call** around him.

 蘇軾 · 王仲儀真贊序："至於緩急之際，決大策，安大眾，呼之即來，揮之即散者，唯世臣巨室為能。"

同義：頤指氣使　Get someone by the short hairs.

mìng zhōng zhù dìng
命中注定
He that is born to be hanged shall never be drowned.

As luck would have it.

例句 ■■ Unfortunately the man was killed in that accident, **he that is born to be hanged shall never be drowned**.

同義：人算不如天算 An ounce of luck is better than a pound of wisdom.
反義：人定勝天 Everyone is the maker of his own fate.

jiù yóu zì qǔ
咎由自取
Asking for troubles.

Lie in the bed one has made.
To be hoisted with one's own petard.
Stew in one's own juice.

例句 ■■ He was punished because he called names in the classroom, **asking for troubles**.

出處 ■■ 尚書：「自作孽。」

同義：自取其咎　Have oneself to blame.

八畫

gù bù zì fēng
固步自封
Get into a groove.

Stay put.
He that stays in the valley shall never get over the hill.
Stand pat.

例句 ✎ ▪▪ To **get into groove** in reasoning will not help us in finding out the truth.

同義：裹足不前　At a standstill.

反義：衝破藩籬　Kick over the traces.

gù ruò jīn tāng
固若金湯
As firm as a rock.

例句 ✎ ▪▪ He will stick to his stand which is **as firm as a rock**.

出處 📖 ▪▪ 漢書："皆為金城湯池，不可攻也。"

同義：安如泰山　Safe upon the solid rock.

反義：不堪一擊
The earthen pot must keep clear of the brass vessel.

gù zhí jǐ jiàn

固執己見

Abide by one's opinion.

Stick to one's gun.
Take the bit in one's teech.
Have a will of one's own.
Nail one's colours to the mast.

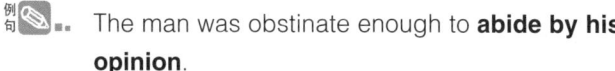 The man was obstinate enough to **abide by his opinion**.

出處 宋史・陳宓傳：“固執己見，動失人心。”

同義：剛愎自用	Reckon without one's host.
反義：收回成命	Eat one's words.

yè láng zì dà

夜郎自大

A humble-bee in a cow-turd thinks himself a king.

To be too long for one's boots.
To be full of oneself.
Every sprat nowadays calls itself a herring.

例句 The guy, like **a humble-bee in a cow-turd thinks himself a king**, gave orders around.

八畫

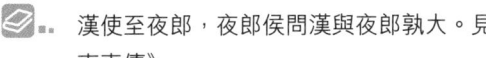
漢使至夜郎，夜郎侯問漢與夜郎孰大。見《漢書·西南夷傳》

> **同義**：自高自大　Think no small beer of oneself.

> **反義**：妄自菲薄　Make oneself too cheap.

wěi mǐ bú zhèn
委靡不振
Get one's tail down.

Feel(Look)blue.
In low spirits.
Down in the dumps.

例句 ■■ Robert had little sleep last night. He **gets his tail down** at his desk now.

出處 ■■ 馬永卿輯·元城先生語錄："至嘉佑末年，天下之事似乎舒緩，委靡不振。"

> **同義**：沒精打采
> With the wind taken out of one's sails.

> **反義**：精神抖擻　Keep one's pecker up.

shān shān lái chí

姍姍來遲

Kiss the hare's foot.

Arrive in an armchair.
At the eleventh hour.

 Good news always **kisses the hare's foot**.

 漢書‧外戚傳："立而望之，何姍姍其來遲。"

> **反義：**爭先恐後　The devil takes the hindmost.

shǐ zhōng bù yú

始終不渝

Not to be shaken.

Dogged adherence.
Keep it up.
Stick to it.

 He will carry out his plan, **not to be shaken** by anything.

八畫

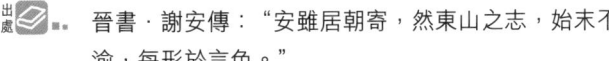
^出_處 ■ 晉書·謝安傳："安雖居朝寄，然東山之志，始末不渝，每形於言色。"

同義：堅持到底　Hold out.	

反義：半途而廢　Do things by halves.	

gū zhù yí zhì
孤注一擲
Bet one's bottom dollar on.

Put all one's eggs in one basket.
Win the horse or lose the saddle.

^例_句 ■ Robert **bets his bottom dollar on** the horse he is sure to win.

^出_處 ■ 元史·伯顏傳："今日我宋天下，猶賭博孤注，輸贏在此一擲耳。"

同義：盡此一舉　Shoot one's bolt.	

反義：留有一手　Have a second string to one's bow.	

gū lòu guǎ wén

孤陋寡聞

Who does not mix with the crowd knows nothing.

例句 His opinion shows us that he is the man **who does not mix with the crowd knows nothing**.

出處 禮記・學記：〝獨學而無友，則孤陋而寡聞。〞

同義：一無所知　To be in the dark.
反義：消息靈通　Have an ear to the ground.

qū zhǐ kě shǔ

屈指可數

A sprinkling.

A handful.
To be on the map.

例句 Honest persons are **a sprinkling** in the world.

出處 歐陽修・唐安公美政頌：〝今文化之盛，其書屈指可數者，無三四人。〞

同義：寥若晨星　Few and far between.
反義：恆河沙數　As numberless as the sands.

八畫

jū ān sī wéi

居安思危

The way to be safe is never to feel secure.

 It is wise to buy fire insurance for your house, **the way to be safe is never to feel secure**.

 左傳・襄十一年："居安思危,思則有備,有備無患。"

同義:宜將有日思無日

In fair weather prepare for foul.

---

suǒ xiàng pī mǐ

所向披靡

To carry all before one.

Nothing stands in one's way.

 He **carried all before him** in the athletic field.

 漢書:"漢軍皆披靡。"

同義:如入無人之境　It was just a walk over.

反義:潰不成軍　To be put to rout.

---

zhāo bīng mǎi mǎ

招兵買馬

Beat up for recruits.

To beef up
Muster up a force.
Raise an army.

 The company is **beating up for recruits** for its new branch.

明 · 無名氏 · 白免記：“到了鄭州，岳節度使在那裏招兵買馬。”

yì rú fǎn zhǎng

易如反掌

As easy as winking (shelling peas).

As easy as pie.
As easy as rolling off a log.
Mere child's play.
I would do it before breakfast.
As easy as A B C.

八
畫

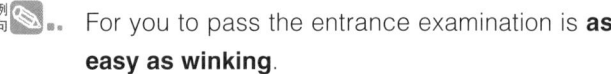

例句 ■■ For you to pass the entrance examination is **as easy as winking**.

出處 ■■ 枚乘‧上書諫吳王："變所欲為，易於反掌，安如泰山。"

同義：輕而易舉　Can do it on one's head.
反義：老大難　A hard nut to crack.

míng mù zhāng dǎn
明目張膽

To brazen it out.

Before one's very eyes.
Under one's very nose.

例句 ■■ He told lies in a **brazening it out** way.

出處 ■■ 唐書："丈夫當敢言地，須要明目張膽，以報天子，焉能碌碌保妻子耶。"

同義：肆無忌憚　To scruple at nothing.
反義：暗中行事　Under the rose.

míng zhé bǎo shēn

明哲保身

Think much, speak little, and write less.

A good name is sooner lost than won.
Be worldly wise and play safe.
Look to one's laurels.

例句 ■■ **Think much, speak little, and write less** will keep you out of trouble.

出處 ■■ 詩經‧大雅‧烝民：〝既明且哲，以保其身。〞

> **反義**：置生死於度外　Heedless of consequences.

míng zhū àn tóu

明珠暗投

To hide one's light under a bushel.

Cast pearls before swine.

例句 ■■ A talented boy must not **hide his light under a bushel**.

出處 ■■ 史記‧魯仲連鄒陽列傳：〝臣聞明月之珠，夜光之璧，以暗投人於道路，人無不按劍目眄者，何則，無因而至前也。〞

八畫

> **同義**：對牛彈琴
>
> It is lost labour to play a jig to an old cat.

míng chá qiū háo

明察秋毫

Capable of keen perception.

See through a millstone.

 The judge, **capable of keen perception,** sentenced the thief to jail.

 孟子 · 梁惠王上： "明足以察秋毫之末。"

> **同義**：歷歷在目　A commanding view.
>
> **反義**：視而不見　As blind as a bat.

péng bǐ wéi jiān

朋比為奸

Play into each other's hands.

Gang up with
Thick as thieves.

In collusion with
To be hand and glove with

例句 They ganged up, **playing into each other's hands**, to cheat their boss.

出處 新唐書·李絳傳：「趨利之人，常為朋比，同其私也。」

> **同義：**狼狽為奸　In cahoots with

dōng shān zài qǐ
東山再起
Stage a comeback.

Bob up like a cork.
He that falls today may rise tomorrow.

例句 The actress **staged a comeback** with her leading role in that movie.

出處 晉書：「謝安初隱東山，後入朝，位登台輔。」

> **同義：**重整旗鼓　Dig up the hatchet.
>
> **反義：**一敗塗地　Down and out.

八畫

wǎng fèi xīn jī
枉費心機

To be a fool for one's pains.

Make a silk purse of a sow's ear.
Go on a wild goose chase.

例句 ■ One **is a fool for one's pains** if one really think he can hitch his wagon to a star.

出處 ■ 元曲選 · 隔江鬥智："你使着這般科段,敢可也枉用心機。"

同義:白費氣力　Wash a blackamoor white.

xīn xīn xiàng róng
欣欣向榮

Flourish like the green bay-tree.

例句 ■ Business of the shop is **flourishing like the green bay- tree**.

出處 ■ 陶潛 · 歸去來辭:"木欣欣以向榮,泉涓涓而始流。"

同義:雨後春筍　Spring up like mushrooms.

xīn xǐ ruò kuáng

欣喜若狂

Leap with joy.

Go into raptures.
Franctic (mad, wild) with joy.
To be on cloud nine.

例句 ✏ ▪▪ We **leap with joy** to know that you are coming.

同義：雀躍三百　Jump for joy.
反義：悲痛欲絕　Torn with grief.

gū míng diào yù

沽名釣譽

Fish for compliments.

Angle for praise.
Court publicity.
Seek the limelight.

例句 ✏ ▪▪ Jack made concessions to **fish for compliments**.

出處 ✏ ▪▪ 荊釵記傳奇：〝妾今移心改嫁，前日投江，乃沽名釣譽也。〞

同義：嘩眾取寵　Impress people by claptrap.

zhān zhān zì xǐ

沾沾自喜

Hug one's self.

Pat oneself on the back.
Lick one's chops.

 Tom **hugged himself** on his success.

 史記 · 魏其侯竇嬰傳："魏其者,沾沾自喜,多易,難以為相。"

反義:快快不樂　Have the blues.

---

wù yǐ lèi jù

物以類聚

Birds of a feather flock together.

Like draws to like.

 They are always together in the bar, both drink like fish, **birds of a feather flock together**.

 周易 · 繫辭："方以類聚,物以羣分。"

同義:人以羣分
A man is known by the company he keeps.

---

wù jí bì fǎn

物極必反

Extreme right is extreme wrong.

Extremes meet.
Too much good fortune is bad fortune.
A flow will have an ebb.
The tide never goes out so far but it always comes in again.

 He went too far too corret what was a minor mistake, and as **extreme right is extreme wrong**, he destroyed the organization.

 鶡冠子・環流："物極則反，命日環流。"

wán huǒ zì fén

玩火自焚

Play with fire (edge tools).

It is ill jesting with edged tools.
He that mischief hatcheth mischief catcheth.
Put your finger into the fire, and they say it was your misfortune.

 To act against the wish of the majority is **playing with fire**.

八畫

出處 ■▪ 左傳 · 隱四年："夫兵，猶火也，弗戢，將自焚也。"

> **反義：**懲羹吹齏　A burnt child dreads the fire.

zhí yán bú huì
直言不諱

From the bottom of one's heart.

Speak one's mind.
Call a spade a spade.
Speak the truth and shame the devil.
Own up readily.
Without reserve.
Straight from the shoulder.

例句 ■▪ As a true friend of yours, I give my opinion **from the bottom of my heart**.

出處 ■▪ 左傳疏："至於制作經典，則直言不諱。"

> **同義：**開門見山　Come straight to the point.

> **反義：**半吞半吐　To mince matters.

zhī nán ér tuì

知難而退

To back out.

To cut a loss.
Shrink back.

例句 ■■ After learning the difficulties involved in the deal, John **backed out**.

出處 ■■ 左傳：「見可而進，知難而退。」

> **反義**：勉為其難　Make the best of a bad bargain.

fèi fǔ zhī yán

肺腑之言

Speak one's conscience.

例句 ■■ I am **speaking my conscience** to you in giving you my suggestion.

出處 ■■ 史記：「田蚡以肺腑為京師相。」

> **同義**：披肝瀝膽　Lay bare one's heart.

八畫

wò xīn cháng dǎn
臥薪嘗膽
Go through thick and thin.

To nurse vengeance.

 I must **go through thick and thin** to accomplish the work trusted to me.

 蘇軾·擬孫權答曹操書:"僕受遺以來,臥薪嘗膽。"

同義: 刻苦鍛煉　Go through the hoop.

hǔ tóu shé wěi
虎頭蛇尾
Going up like a rocket and coming down like a stick.

Come out at the little end of the horn.
The mountain has brought forth a mouse.
In like a lion, out like a lamb.
A flash in the pan.

 He accepted the job at the beginning but **going up like a rocket and coming down like a stick**, he backed out after learning that it was not an easy job.

出處 元曲選‧李逵負荊：“這廝敢狗行狼心，虎頭蛇尾。”

> **同義**：來如風雨，去似微塵
> He who swells in prosperity will shrink in adversity.

> **反義**：始終不渝　Keep it up.

chū chū máo lú
初出茅廬
A raw recruit.

A green horn.
A freshwater sailor.
As green as grass.
Wet behind the ears.

例句 He is **a raw recruit** who knows little about our trade.

> **同義**：少不更事　Not dry behind the ears.

> **反義**：老於世故　Know which way the wind blows.

八畫

chū shēng zhī dú bú wèi hǔ
初生之犢不畏虎

They that know nothing fear nothing.

例句
.. Members of the team played against the Giants boldly – **they that know nothing fear nothing**.

出處
.. 三國演義："俗云，初生之犢不畏虎。"

> **反義**：驚弓之鳥　A burned child dreads the fire.

fǎn lǎo huán tóng
返老還童

In one's second childhood.

An old man is twice a child.

例句
.. Leonard joined the football team at the age of sixty, he was then **in his second childhood**.

出處
.. 神仙傳："八公曰，王薄我老，今則少矣，八公皆變為童子。"

> **反義**：年少老成　An old head on young shoulders.

jìn shuǐ lóu tái xiān dé yuè

近水樓台先得月

The parson always christens his own child first.

例句 He got the firsthand information direct from his boss as **the parson always christens his own child first**.

出處 俞文豹‧清夜錄：“近水樓台先得月，向陽花木易為春。”

同義：近廚得食 A baker's wife may bite of a bun, a brewer's wife may drink of a tun.
反義：遠水不救近火 Water afar off quencheth not fire.

jìn zài zhǐ chǐ

近在咫尺

Within calling distance.

Hard by.
Just round the corner.
Two whoops and a holler.
Near at hand.

八畫

My office is **within calling distance** from your's.

 蘇軾·杭州謝上表："凜然威光,近在咫尺。"

> **反義**:天涯海角　Ends of the earth.

jìn zhū zhě chì jìn mò zhě hēi
近朱者赤,近墨者黑
Touch pitch, and you will be defiled.

He who lies down with dogs will rise with fleas.
Who keeps company with the wolf will learn to howl.
Keep not ill men company lest you increse the
　　number.

 The boy played the game machine as all his
schoolmates did, **touching pitch and one will
be defiled**.

 傅玄·太子少傅箴："近朱者赤,近墨者黑。"

> **同義**:染於蒼則蒼,染於黃則黃
> 　　　　The finger that touches rouge will be red.

jīn yù liáng yán

金玉良言

Good advice is beyond price.

 Do listen to your teacher's words, **good advice is beyond price**.

> **同義：**醍醐灌頂　Give a person a rub of the thumb.

> **反義：**廢話　Stuff and nonsense.

jīn yù qí wài bài xù qí zhōng

金玉其外，敗絮其中

A stuff shirt.

All that glitters in not gold.
Whited sepulchres, which indeed appear beautiful
outward, but are within full of dead man's bones.

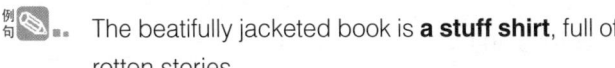 The beatifully jacketed book is **a stuff shirt**, full of rotten stories.

劉基 · 誠意伯集 · 賣柑者言：「又何往而不金玉其外，敗絮其中也哉。」

> **同義：**繡花枕頭　Fair without and foul within.

八畫

cháng qū zhí rù

長驅直入

It was just a walk over.

 It was just a walk over for the army to take that castle.

 曹操‧勞徐晃令："所聞古之善用兵者,未有長驅直入敵圍者也。"

同義:勢如破竹

Like a hot knife cutting through butter.

反義:到處碰壁　Driven from pillar to post.

---

yǔ guò tiān qíng

雨過天晴

Change for the better.

After rain comes fine weather.
After rain comes sunshine.
The sorst is over.

 His condition is alright now as his illness has **changed for the better**.

出處 ■■ 謝在杭文海披沙記：「雨過天青雲破處，這般顏色做將來。」

> **反義**：山雨欲來風滿樓
> When the clouds are upon the hills they'll
> come down by the mills.

qīng chū yú lán
青出於藍

The scholar may excel the master.

Get ahead of.

例句 ■■ Emerson did much better in his field than his
teacher, **the scholar may excel the master**.

出處 ■■ 荀子・勸學：「青取之於藍而青於藍。」

> **同義**：盲拳打死老師傅
> The scholar may worst the master.
>
> **反義**：不堪造就　Ill beef never made good broth.

八畫

fēi tóng xiǎo kě
非同小可
Something out of the ordinary.

No small matter.
Not to be dismissed lightly.

 The discovery made by him is **something out of the ordinary**.

 元曲選 · 魔合羅："人命事關天關地,非同小可。"

同義:不可輕視　Not to be sneezed at.
反義:平淡無奇　Nothing to write home about.

xìn kǒu kāi hé
信口開河
Speak off the top of one's head.

Shoot off one's mouth.
To talk without thinking is to shoot without aiming.
Talk at random.

 He **spoke off the top of his head** about his work in the past.

元曲選‧爭報恩："那妮子一尺水翻騰做一丈波，怎當他只留支剌，信口開河。"

> **反義：**守口如瓶　As close as an oyster.

xìn kǒu cí huáng
信口雌黃
Talk through one's hat.

Speak through the back of one's neck.
With a tongue too long for one's teeth.
Talk glibly.

 Don't take his words as he is **talking through his hat**.

 晉‧孫盛‧晉陽秋："王衍能言，於意有不安者，輒更易之，時號口中雌黃。"

> **同義：**大放厥詞　To let oneself loose.

> **反義：**引經據典　Speak by the book.

cù xī tán xīn

促膝談心

Get knee to knee with one.

Have a heart-to-heart talk.
Take into confidence.

 It is always good to **get knee to knee with a good friend**.

> **同義：**推心置腹　From the bottom of one's heart.
>
> **反義：**話不投機半句多
> It's ill talking between a full man and a fasting.

qián gōng jìn qì

前功盡棄

Go down the drain.

Have all the troubles for nothing.
All labour lost.

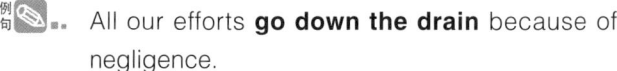 All our efforts **go down the drain** because of negligence.

五代史補："今一旦反作脱空漢，前功盡棄，令公之心安乎。"

同義： 功虧一簣　Look back from the plough.

反義： 練出功夫
He that shoots oft shall at last hit the mark.

成語故事： Happy is the country that has no history

　　沒有歷史的國家是幸福的國家，這是孟德斯鳩說的名句。如果我們認識到歷史只是人類的悲劇與罪惡的記錄，那麼沒有歷史的國家就是沒有這種記錄的、幸福的國家了。英國歷史學家 Thomas Carlyle（1795-1881，著有"法國革命"、"論英雄、英雄崇拜和歷史上的英雄事蹟"等著作）曾引用孟德斯鳩此語。此語亦作：Happy the people whose annals are blank in history。看來歷史悠久並非幸福之國了。

qián yīn hòu guǒ

前因後果

What brings about.

Cause and effect.

 What brings about the success is your diligence.

 南齊書‧高逸傳論：" 今樹以前因，報以後果。"

qián chē zhī jiàn

前車之鑒

In doing we learn.

Learn wisdom by the follies of others.
Wise men learn by other men's mistakes

 In doing we learn, we took his fault as a lesson and avoided the same mistake.

 賈誼‧治安策：" 諺曰，前車覆，後車誡。"

同義：前事不忘，後事之師
Repent what's past, avoid what is to come.

九
畫

qián chéng sì jǐn

前程似錦

Have a brilliant prospect.

To have the world before one.
To have the ball at one's feet.

 You **have a brilliant prospect** with your fine scholastic achievement.

同義：錦繡前程	Promising future.
反義：日暮途窮	Driven to the last extremity.

yǒng wǎng zhí qián

勇往直前

Forge ahead.

Go well up to the bridle.

 I **forged ahead** quickly to win the race.

同義：一往無前	Press forward.
反義：臨陣退縮	Turn tail at the last moment.

bó rán dà nù

勃然大怒

Go black in the face.

Fly into a rage.
Fly off the handle.
Hit the ceiling.
Flare up.
Go off the top.

 The boss **goes black in the face** while reading the report.

同義：大發雷霆　Explode with rage.
反義：啞然失笑　Burst out laughing.

nán yuán běi zhé

南轅北轍

Look one way and row another.

Poles apart.
Diametrically opposite.
East is East and West is West.

 For a smoker to talk about lung cancer is to **look one way and row another**.

出處 ■■ 戰國策‧魏策四：〝南轅北轍，猶至楚而北行也。〞

同義：背道而馳　Run counter to
反義：殊途同歸　Extremes meet.

hòu yán wú chǐ
厚顏無恥
Have plenty of cheek.

As bold as brass.
To brazen out.
Have the effrontery to

例句 ■■ He owes me money yot **has the cheek** to invite so many people to dinner.

出處 ■■ 孔稚圭‧北山移文：〝豈可使芳杜厚顏，薜荔蒙恥。〞

同義：恬不知恥　Have no sense of shame.
反義：羞人答答　Feel like thirty cents.

yǎo wén jiáo zì
咬文嚼字
To be pedantic.

Use flowery words.
To speak holiday.
To have swallowed the dictionary.
Talk like a book.
Chop logic.

 When you talk about daily life, do not **be pedantic** like an old scholar.

 元曲選 · 殺狗勸夫：" 使不的你咬文嚼字。"

同義：句斟字酌　Weigh one's words.
反義：信口開河　Shoot off one's mouth.

chuí tóu sàng qì
垂頭喪氣
Hang one's head.

Down in the mouth (dumps).
With one's tail between one's legs.
Look crestfallen.

Robert **hangs his head** down because he lost in the competition.

 唐書： "失勢者垂頭喪氣。"

同義：沒精打采
With the wind taken out of one's sails.

反義：趾高氣揚　Ride the high horse.

hòu lái jū shàng

後來居上

The best is behind.

He finished first though he began last.

 He started the last and became the first to find **the best is behind**.

 史記·汲鄭列傳： "陛下用羣臣，如積薪耳，後來者居上。"

同義：迎頭趕上　To overtake one.

反義：遙遙領先　Streets ahead of

nù bù kě è
怒不可遏
To boil over.

To hit the roof.
Beside oneself with rage.
To be in a fume.

 The boss **boiled over** when he found that we have overrun the budget.

同義：暴跳如雷　In a towering rage.
反義：心平氣和　Compose oneself.

nù fà chōng guān
怒髮衝冠
Have one's dander up.

Bristle with anger.
To lose one's hair.
Mad as a hatter.
To be in a towering rage.
Flip one's lid.
Blow one's top.

Just hearing about the crime was enough to **have one's dander up**.

 史記‧藺相如傳：「相如視秦王無意償趙城，因持璧卻立倚柱，怒髮衝冠。」

> **同義**：令人髮指　Make one's hair stand on end.

> **反義**：喜形於色
> A merry heart makes a cheerful countenance.

jí zhōng shēng zhì

急中生智

Necessity is the mother of invention.

In a flash of inspiration.

 He used the Scotch tape as bandaid, **necessity is the mother of invention**.

> **同義**：心生一計　Hit upon an idea.

> **反義**：無計可施　Up the creek without a paddle.

成語故事：Necessity is the mother of invention

"伊索寓言"中有"烏鴉和水罐"（The Crow and the Pitcher）的故事：一隻烏鴉口渴想飲水罐中的水，可是喝不到，後來想到啣石子掉進水罐中去，喝到了上溢的

水。寓言的結尾就是這句話：需要乃發明之母。此句中的 Necessity 和 mother 並舉，將前者擬人化，又稱之謂"智慧之師"（teacher of wit），利器發明者（inventor of good things）以及生產之母（mother of productions）。這樣的擬人化，始於十六世紀期間。

jí gōng jìn lì

急功近利

Better an egg today than a hen tomorrow.

Better keep now than seek anon.
A bird in hand is worth two in the bush.
One today is worth two tomorrow.

例句 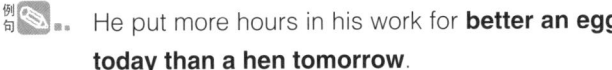 He put more hours in his work for **better an egg today than a hen tomorrow**.

yuàn tiān yóu rén

怨天尤人

Complain of one's lot.

Everyone puts his faults on the times.
Say the devil's paternoster.
A bad workman always blames his tools.

例句 ▪▪ One should do one's best and know it's in vain to
complain of one's lot.

出處 ▪▪ 論語 · 憲問： "不怨天，不尤人。"

> **反義**：樂天知命　The world is his that enjoys it.

huǎng rán dà wù

恍然大悟

It dawned upon one.

See daylight.

例句 ▪▪ When John learned the fact, **it drawned upon him**
that he was cheated.

> **同義**：如夢初醒　To wake up to

> **反義**：如入五里霧中　To be lost in the cloud.

tián bù zhī chǐ
恬不知恥
Thick-skinned.

Have the effrontery (face) to
Have no sense of shame.

 Jack is so **thick-skinned** that he cheated in the examination.

 馮贄・雲仙雜記："倪芳飲後，必有狂怪，恬然不恥。"

同義：厚顏無恥　Have plenty of cheek.
反義：於心有愧　Have a guilty conscience.

àn bīng bú dòng
按兵不動
Stay one's hand.

Bide one's time.
To mark time.

 He was very much excited, but she asked him to **stay at his hand** before taking any action.

 史記："王按兵毋出。"

àn bù jiù bān

按部就班

In apple-pie order.

A place for everything, and everything in its place.

例句 ▪▪ No hurry, let's carry out the plan **in apple-pie order**.

出處 ▪▪ 文選·陸機文賦："然後選義按部，老辭就班。"

同義： 井井有條　Keep everything ship-shape.
反義： 亂作一團　All in a huddle.

shì mù yǐ dài

拭目以待

Wait and see.

It remains to be seen.

例句 ▪▪ Let's **wait and see** how the government will handle the problem.

出處 ▪▪ 漢書："天下莫不拭目傾耳。"

同義： 風物長宜放眼量 See which way the cat jumps.

chí zhī yǐ héng

持之以恆

Stick to it.

Keep it up.
Without a break.
Perseverance will prevail.

例句 ✍ ■■ If you are on diet, **stick to it** at least for a month.

同義：滴水穿石 　　　　Constant dripping wears away the stone.
反義：三天打魚，兩天曬網　By fits and starts.

zhǐ lù wéi mǎ

指鹿為馬

Talk black into white.

Swear black is white.

例句 ✍ ■■ This Johnson is not that Johnson, don't **talk black into white**.

出處 ✍ ■■ 史記："趙高持鹿獻於二世曰，馬也。"

反義：丁是丁，卯是卯　Call a spade a spade.

tiāo bō lí jiàn

挑撥離間

Stir the coals.

Breed bad blood.
Sow dissension.
Play off one against the other.
Drive a wedge between
Set people at loggerheads.
Set people together by the ears.

 The congressman tried to **stir the coals** among parties by his latest speech.

同義：惹事生非　Stir up trouble.	
反義：排難解紛　Pour oil on troubled waters.	

gù tài fù méng

故態復萌

Return to one's old habit.

Back in the old rut.
At one's little games again.
Return to one's vomit.
He that has done ill once will do it again.
Fall from grace.

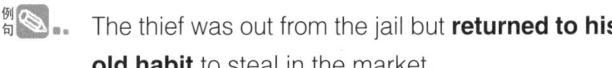
例句 ■■ The thief was out from the jail but **returned to his old habit** to steal in the market.

出處 ■■ 後漢書：" 帝曰，狂奴故態也。"

同義：賊性難改　Once a knave and ever a knave.

反義：改過自新　Turn over a new leaf.

xīng huǒ liáo yuán
星火燎原
Little chips light great fire.

例句 ■■ Don't overlook that disturbance, **little chips light great fire**.

出處 ■■ 書經・盤庚上：" 若火之燎於原，不可向邇。"

liú fāng bǎi shì
流芳百世
Leave one's mark on history.

Have a niche in the temple of fame.

例
句
James's heroic action will **leave his mark on history**.

出
處
世説新語：“晉桓溫有大志，嘗撫枕歎日，既不能流芳百世，不足復遺臭萬年耶。”

同義：萬古流芳　On the scroll of fame.

反義：遺臭萬年
The evil that men do lives after them.

liú lián wàng fǎn
流連忘返
Held spellbound by

Can't tear oneself away,
linger on.

例
句
The travellers are **held spellbound by** the beauty of the West lake.

出
處
孟子·梁惠王下：“從流下而忘反謂之流，從流上而忘反謂之連。”

反義：溜之大吉　Make oneself scarce.

jīn jīn yǒu wèi
津津有味
Smack one's lips.

Lick one's chops.
With gusto (relish).

例句  He **smacked his lips** while testing the new dish in that restaurant yesterday.

> **反義：**味同嚼蠟　Dry as sawdust.

xǐ ěr gōng tīng
洗耳恭聽
Prick up one's ears.

To be all ears.
Strain one's ears.

例句 The student **pricked up his ears** to listen to his teacher's words.

出處 單刀會傳奇："請君侯試說一遍，下官洗耳恭聽。"

> **反義：**充耳不聞　Turn a deaf ear to

wèi shǒu wèi wěi

畏首畏尾

Too much taking heed is loss.

Full of misgivings.
Have cold feet.

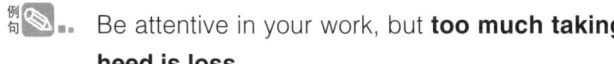 Be attentive in your work, but **too much taking heed is loss**.

左傳·文十七年：〝古人有言曰，畏首畏尾，身其餘幾。〞

同義：膽小如鼠　As timid as a mouse.
反義：敢想敢幹　To shoot one's wad.

xiāng xíng jiàn chù

相形見絀

Can't sustain comparison with.

Cast into the shade.
Pale beside another (by comparison).
Make one shrink small.
Take the shine out of
To be outshone.

例句 ‧‧ Robert's essay **can't sustain comparison with** the one written by James.

> **同義**：小巫見大巫
> The moon is not seen where the sun shines.

xiāng tí bìng lùn
相提並論
Lumped together.

Put in the same class.
Place on a par.

例句 ‧‧ Please don't **lump me together** with other writers.

出處 ‧‧ 史記‧魏其武安侯列傳："相提而論。"

> **反義**：不可同日而語
> Not to be mentioned in the same breath.

qiū fēng sǎo luò yè
秋風掃落葉
Make a clean sweep.

Sweep everything before one.

九畫

 The fire **made a clean sweep** of the village.

 三國志‧魏志‧辛毗傳：〝以明公之威，應困窮之敵，擊疲弊之寇，無異迅風之振秋葉矣。〞

> **同義：**囊括一空　Grand slam.

tū rú qí lái
突如其來
Out of the blue.

A bolt from the blue.
Appear from nowhere.
Sally forth.

 A letter arrived **out of the blue** from a friend in Beijing inviting me to stay with him.

 周易‧離：〝突如其來。〞

> **同義：**出乎意外　Out of one's reckoning.

tū fēi měng jìn
突飛猛進
In seven-league boots.

By leaps and bounds.

Make giant strides.

 Science has advanced **in seven-league boots** in recent days.

> **反義：**蝸牛上樹　At a snail's pace.

měi zhōng bù zú
美中不足
The peacock has fair feathers but foul feet.

There are lees to every wine.
There is no rose without a thorn.
There is no garden without its weeds.

 That black spot on the painting reminds me of **the peacock has fair feathers but foul feet**.

> **反義：**十全十美　The pink of perfection.

bèi xìn qì yì
背信棄義
Go back on a person.

To back out.

九
畫

Play one false.
A breach of promise.
Go back on.

例句 He is a gentleman who will not **go back on anybody**.

> **反義**：忠心耿耿　As true as the dial to the sun.

bèi dào ér chí
背道而馳
Run counter to

Look one way and row another.
To be diametrically opposed to

例句 I'm not to **run counter to** my principle to lend money to that guy.

出處 蘇軾詩："仙山佛國本同歸，世跡玄關兩背馳。"

> **同義**：南轅北轍　Poles apart.

> **反義**：方向對頭　On the right tack.

hú sī luàn xiǎng

胡思亂想

Go off into wild flights of fancy.

Build castles in the air (Spain).
Have a bee in one's bonnet.
To be in the clouds.

 Jack **went off into wild flights of fancy** to think that he could have the hand of that beautiful rich widow.

 朱熹："不要如此胡思亂量，過卻日子也。"

> **同義：**想入非非
> Show him an egg, and instantly the whole air is full of feathers.

hú shuō bā dào

胡說八道

Stuff and nonsense.

Talk through one's hat (the back of one's neck).
Talk twaddle.
Talk rubbish.

 **Stuff and nonsense**! Don't try to fool me.

九畫

反義：引經據典　Give chapter and verse.

ruò yào rén bù zhī chú fēi jǐ mò wéi
若要人不知，除非己莫為
There is a witness everywhere.

What is done by night appears by day.

例句 Don't cheat in examination as it will be discovered –**there is a witness everywhere**.

出處 枚乘・上書諫吳王："欲人不聞，莫若不言，欲人不知，莫若不為。"

反義：偷偷摸摸　On the sly.

ruò wú qí shì
若無其事
Calm and composed.

Cool as a cucumber.
As if nothing has happened.

例句 How can you be so **calm and composed** when you are in such a mess?

| **同義：**行若無事 | With perfect composure. |
| **反義：**煞有介事 | Fuss up and down. |

yīng xióng suǒ jiàn lüè tóng
英雄所見略同
Share the same view.

Great minds think alike.
Great wits jump.
See eye to eye.

 John and James **share the same view** on that subject.

 三國志 · 蜀志 · 龐統傳："天下智謀之士，所見略同耳。"

| **同義：**意見一致 | To be of one mind. |
| **反義：**意見分歧 | Opinions are divided. |

gǒu yán cán chuǎn
苟延殘喘

Keep body and soul together.

Linger on.

例句 ■■ The beggar lives a miserable life just to **keep body and soul together**.

出處 ■■ 馬中錫 · 中山狼傳："今日之事，何不使我得早處囊中，以苟延殘喘乎。"

> **同義**：得過且過　To muddle through.

pò bù dé yǐ
迫不得已

It can't be helped.

Under duress.
Needs must when the devil drives.
Do something under protest.
Have no alternative but to

例句 ■■ **It can't be helped** for me to blame him for our loss.

出處 ■■ 漢書 · 王莽傳上："迫不得已然後受詔。"

同義：不由自主　In spite of oneself.

---

chóng zhěng qí gǔ
重整旗鼓
Dig up the hatchet.

Rally one's forces.
Re-shuffle.

 Don't be discouraged. Let's **dig up the hatchet** and carry on.

---

miàn bù gǎi róng
面不改容
Not to bat an eye.

Without turning a hair.
Keep a straight face.
Face the music.

 The criminal does **not bat an eye** when he tells lies.

同義：泰然自若　With perfect composure.

反義：大驚失色　Jump out of one's skin.

miàn rú tǔ sè

面如土色

Turn pale.

As pale as death.

 Robert's **turned pale** when his secret was exposed.

同義：顏色憔悴　Peak and pine.
反義：滿臉通紅　To colour up.

miàn hóng ěr chì

面紅耳赤

Turn red in the gills.

To colour up.
Flush with shame.
Blush with shyness.
One's ears burn.
As red as fire.
Blush as red as a peony.

 He was so ashamed that he **turned red in the gills**.

同義：滿臉通紅　Flush red all over.

miàn miàn xiāng qù

面面相覷

At a nonplus.

At a loss what to do.

例句  When they were questioned by their teacher, they were **at a nonplus**, not knowing what to say.

出處 李贄 · 焚書因記往事："一旦有警,則面面相覷,絕無人色。"

miàn wú rén sè

面無人色

As white as a sheet.

As pale as a ghost.
Look ashen.
Pale around the gills.

例句 The girl turned **white as a sheet** when she saw the painful scene.

出處 漢書 · 李廣傳："廣為匈奴所敗,吏士皆無人色,廣意氣相若。"

同義:面如土色　Turn pale.	
反義:滿面紅光　As sound as a pippin.	

fēng chí diàn chè
風馳電掣
With lightning speed.

Burn up the road.
Go like a shot.

例句 🖊 ▪▪ The speeding motorcycle passed in front of us **with lightening speed**.

出處 ✒ ▪▪ 六韜・龍韜："風馳電掣，不知所由。"

同義：開足馬力　At full speed.
反義：慢條斯理　At a snail's pace.

fēng chén pú pú
風塵僕僕
Shake off the dust from one's feet.

Travel from place to place.

例句 🖊 ▪▪ A salesman has to **shake off the dust from his feet** all the time.

反義：深居簡出　Live in seclusion.

fēi huáng téng dá

飛黃騰達

Rise in the world.

Flourish like the green bay-tree.
His star was in the ascendant.
Get on in the world.

例句 ■■ The writer is **risen in the world** after the publication
of his new book.

出處 ■■ 韓愈詩：〝飛黃騰踏去，不能顧蟾蜍。〞

同義：平步青雲　Skyrocket to fame.
反義：參差不偶　In a sorry plight.

shǒu dāng qí chōng

首當其衝

Exposed to danger.

Bear the brunt of
Throw oneself into the breach.

例句 ■■ He led the team to win the game, **exposed to
danger** all the time.

出處 ■■ 漢書 · 五行志下之上：〝鄭當其衝，不能修德。〞

同義：一馬當先　To be in the lead.	
反義：避重就輕　To ride off side issues.	

十
畫

chéng fēng pò làng
乘風破浪
Sail before the wind.

Brave the winds and waves.
Carry a bone in the teeth.
Plough the waves.

例句 ■■ His career rises in the world like **sailing before the wind** after he has been promoted.

出處 ■■ 宋書‧宗愨傳．"願乘長風，破萬里浪。"

dào xíng nì shī
倒行逆施
Turn things upside down.

After meat, mustard.
After death, the doctor.
Put the cart before the horse.
Put the clock back.

例句 ■■ To put the cart before the horse is to **turn things upside down**.

出處 ■■ 史記‧伍子胥列傳："吾日暮途遠，吾故倒行而逆施之。"

同義：本末倒置　Turn topsy-turvy.

反義：順應潮流　Go with the tide.

成語故事：Necessity has no law

　　此話直譯作：必要之前無法律。原意指有德之士有時不得不破法行事。古希臘抒情詩人西摩尼得斯 (Simonides，公元前 556-468) 有 "神都不和需要相爭" 之語。古羅馬哲學家柏羅丁 (Plotinus，約計：公元 205-270 年，新柏拉圖學派主要代表) 曾經說過：神都要讓步給必要。由此可見這原是一句老諺語。這話於十四世紀期間傳入英國。

　　克倫威爾 (Oliver Cromwell，1599-1658) 曾在國會演說中引用。

十畫

gāng bì zì yòng
剛愎自用
Stubborn as a mule.

As tough as nails.
Reckon without one's host.
To be a law unto oneself.

 Our boss is **stubbon as a mule**, never takes anyone's advice.

 蘇東坡後集‧謝宣召入學士院狀："知臣剛愎自用，雖有寬饒（蓋寬饒）之狂，察臣招摩不移，庶幾長孺之守。"

反義：不恥下問　Bow down thy ear.

yuán xíng bì lù
原形畢露
Put one's cards on the table.

Show the cloven foot (hoof).
Show one's horns.
Come out in one's true colours.
Have feet of clay.

The confession has **put his cards on the table**.

同義：兇相畢露　Bare one's fangs.
反義：喬裝打扮　Sail under false colours.

chún qiāng shé jiàn
唇槍舌劍
Speak daggers.

Have a sharp tongue.
Exchange heated words.
Break a lance with one.
Cross swords.

 One may **speak daggers** to his contender but never use them.

 元曲選 · 武漢臣 · 玉壺春："使心猿意馬，逞舌劍唇槍。"

hài qún zhī mǎ
害羣之馬
A black sheep.

One scabbed (sickly) sheep infects a whole flock.
The rotten apple injures its neighbour.

Bad egg of the community.

 That naughty boy is the **black sheep** of the family.

 莊子：＂夫為天下，亦奚以異乎牧馬哉，亦去其害馬者而已矣。＂

jiā tú sì bì
家徒四壁
There is not a stick of furniture around.

As poor as a church mouse.

 He is so poor that **there is not a stick of furniture around** in his place.

 漢書・司馬相如傳：＂文君夜亡奔相如，相如與馳歸成都，家徒四壁立。＂

同義：一無所有 Not a shirt to one's name.
反義：家財萬貫 Have money to burn.

jiā yù hù xiǎo
家喻戶曉
Pass from mouth to mouth.

On everyone's lips.

Common knowledge.
To be a household word.
To be in everyone's mouth.
Every barber knows that.
The talk of the town.

 His bad name **passed from mouth to mouth** in his native town.

 宣和畫譜："不出九重深邃之地，使四方萬里朝令夕行，豈家至而戶曉也哉。"

> **同義：**膾炙人口　Enjoy great popularity.

róng guāng huàn fā
容光煥發
Shine like a shittim barn door.

One's face brightens up.
One's face glows with health.
To be in the pink.
In radiant health.

 The old man is **shinning like a shittim barn door** at the age of eighty.

同義：滿面紅光	Glowing with health.
反義：面無人色	As pale as a ghost.

ruò ròu qiáng shí

弱肉強食

Jungle justice.

The weakest goes to the wall.
Survival of the fittest.

例句 ▪▪ The landlord, in **jungle justice**, grabbed the harvest from his tenants.

出處 ▪▪ 韓愈‧送浮屠文暢師序：〝弱之肉，強之食。〞

同義：大魚吃小魚
The little cannot be great unless he devours many.

tú láo wú gōng

徒勞無功

A waste of effort.

A wild goose chase.

Shoe the goose.

Make ropes of sand.

Plow the sands and sow the waves.

Fruitless labour.

Beat one's head against a wall.

 It's **a waste of effort** to ask for a raise when the business is not so good.

同義：枉費心機　To be a fool for one's pains.

反義：練出功夫

He that shoots oft shall at last hit the mark.

---

huǐ guò zì xīn

悔過自新

To be on the cot.

Make a fresh start.

Turn over a new leaf.

 Jack **is on the cot** and starts his new career, putting his criminal record behind.

 唐書 · 馮元常傳："劍南有光火盜，元常喻以恩信，約悔過自新。"

同義：改邪歸正　To mend one's way.	
反義：堅決不改　To sit tight.	

tǐng shēn ér chū

挺身而出

Take the initiative.

Stand in the gap.
Stick up for
Gaze at the melody.

例句　．． John **took the initiative** for the labour union to bargain with the boss.

出處　．． 元‧王實甫‧西廂記：〝小生挺身而出，作書與杜將軍。〞

反義：躲躲閃閃　Wriggle like a cut snake.

shí lái yùn zhuǎn

時來運轉

Take a turn for the better.

The turn of the tide.

Better luck next time.
The worse luck now, the better another time.

 John got a new job, **taking a turn for the better**.

xǔ xǔ rú shēng
栩栩如生
A speaking likeness.

True to life.

 The sculpture carries **a speaking likeness** of the look of the hero.

 莊子・齊物論："昔者莊周夢為胡蝶,栩栩然胡蝶也。"

gé gé bú rù
格格不入
Not talk the same language.

Go against the grain with one.
Out of keeping with
A square peg in a round hole.

例句 ■■ When discussing philosophy, we are **not talking the same language**.

出處 ■■ 禮記・學記：〝發然後禁，則扞格而不勝，時過然後學，則勤苦而難成。〞

同義：話不投機半句多
　　　　It's ill taking between a full man and a fasting.

反義：氣味相投　Birds of a feather flock together.

---

shū tú tóng guī
殊途同歸
All roads lead to Rome.

Extremes meet.

例句 ■■ Tourists all come to visit Hong Kong as **all roads lead to Rome**.

出處 ■■ 周易・繫辭下：〝天下同歸而殊途，一致而百慮。〞

同義：百川歸海
　　　　All rivers do what they can for the sea.

反義：分道揚鑣　To part company.

qì wèi xiāng tóu
氣味相投
Hit it off well.

Like draws to like.
Like will to like.
Birds of a feather flock together.

 As soon as they met, they **hit it off well**.

> **同義**：格格不入　Out of keeping with.

qì jí bài huài
氣急敗壞
To be worked up.

Gasping for breath.
Get into wax.

 Jack **was worked up** and came in for help.

> **反義**：心平氣和　Keep cool

láng tūn hǔ yàn

狼吞虎嚥

Eat like a horse.

Have a wolf in one's stomach.
Make a pig of oneself.
Eat one's head off.
Polish of a meal.
Make a beast of oneself.
Gobble up.
Garbage down.

例
句 He is very hungry, **eating like a horse**.

同義：大快朵頤　Gorge oneself.
反義：淺斟低酌 　　　　Eat at pleasure, drink by measure.

láng bèi bù kān

狼狽不堪

One shoe off and one shoe on.

All in a fluster.

In a pretty fix (tight corner).
Helter-skelter.
In an embarrassing situation (awkward predicament).
To be caught with one's pants down.

 I am **one shoe off and one shoe on** because I have to work late and we have guests for early dinner at home.

 李密‧陳情表：〝臣之進退，實為狼狽。〞

同義：處境尷尬　To be in a pretty pickle.
反義：從容不迫　Take things easy.

jí fēng zhī jìng cǎo
疾風知勁草

Oaks may fall when reeds stand the storm.

The good seaman is known in bad weather.

 John sticks it out as the old saying goes: **Oaks may fall when reeds stand the storm**.

 宋書：〝故疾風知勁草，嚴霜知貞木。〞

同義：路遙知馬力
A good seaman is known in bad weather.

pò tì wéi xiào

破涕為笑

They that sow in tears shall reap in joy.

Nothing dries sooner than a tear.
Sadness and gladness succeed each other.

例
句
On learning that his home is safe in the fire, John smiled, **they that sow in tears shall reap in joy**.

出
處
劉琨‧答盧諶書："時復相與舉觴對膝，破涕為笑。"

> **反義**：樂極生悲
> He that talk much of his happiness summons grief.

pò fǔ chén zhōu

破釜沉舟

Go for broke.

Burn one's boats (bridges).

例
句
I decided to **go for broke** to carry out the plan.

出
處
項羽："皆沉船，破釜甑。"

> **同義**：背城借一　Fight to the last ditch.

shén bù shǒu shè

神不守舍

Lose one's presence of mind.

One's heart leaps into one's mouth.
To be harum-scarum.
Quite absent-minded.

 Jack seems to have **lost his presence of mind** in his work.

同義：心不在焉　To be day-dreaming.
反義：全神貫注　Focus one's attention on

shén bù zhī guǐ bù jué

神不知，鬼不覺

Behind one's back.

On the sly.
By stealth.
On tip-toe.

 He told lies about me **behind my back**.

元曲選 · 爭報恩："恁做事可甚人不知鬼不覺。"

同義：偷偷摸摸　Up to some hangky-pangky.

shén cǎi yì yì

神采奕奕

Fresh as a daisy.

Full of pep (beans).
As fit as a fiddle.
Hale and hearty.
Look like a million dollars.

例句 Helen looks as **fresh as a daisy** today.

同義：英姿煥發　In one's vigorous youth.
反義：沒精打采　In the dumps.

xiào lǐ cáng dāo

笑裏藏刀

Velvet paws hide sharp claws.

Feline amenities.
Stab one in the back.
To be nasty-nice.

例句 Don't trust that guy. He speaks well but **velvet paws hide sharp claws**.

出處 水滸傳："林沖道，這是笑裏藏刀，言清行濁的人。"

> **同義：**口蜜腹劍　A honey tongue, a heart of gall.
>
> **反義：**心地光明
> Have one's heart in the right place.

sù mèi píng shēng
素昧平生
A total stranger.

Haven't had the pleasure of meeting one.
Not to know one from Adam.

例句 ■■ Tom was **a total stranger** to me when we first met in Shanghai.

出處 ■■ 李商隱・贈田叟詩："交親得路昧平生。"

> **反義：**深知底細
> Know the length of a person's foot.

xiōng yǒu chéng zhú
胸有成竹
Have an ace up one's sleeve.

Have more than one string to one's bow.
Know the ropes.

The problem does not worry John as he **has an ace up in his sleeve** to deal with it.

 晁補之 · 雞肋集： "與可畫竹時，胸中有成竹。"

同義：心中有數　Know one's own mind.
反義：一籌莫展　To be at one's wit's end.

xiōng wú diǎn mò
胸無點墨
A numskull.

Not to know A from a windmill.

 His vague words show us that he is **a numskull**.

同義：目不識丁　Not to know B from a bull's foot.
反義：滿腹經綸　To give chapter and verse.

néng qū néng shēn
能屈能伸
Stretch your legs according to your coverlet.

Fit in.
Do in Rome as the Romans do.

例句 ■■ I don't mind even if the assignment is a demotion as you should be able to **stretch your legs according to your coverlet**.

> **反義**：高不成，低不就
> He that will not stoop for a pin shall never be worth a pound.

cǎo mù jiē bīng
草木皆兵
Take every bush for a bugbear.

Fields have eyes, and woods have ears.
Afraid of one's own shadow.

例句 ■■ The defeated soldiers are so frightened that they **take every bush for a bugbear**.

出處 ■■ 東晉書："堅登城望八公山上，草木皆類人形。"

nì lái shùn shòu
逆來順受
What can't be cured must be endured.

If you don't like it, you can lump it.
Grin and bear it.
Swallow one's pride.

Put up with it.

Take it lying down.

Make a virtue of necessity.

Make the best of it.

Take something in good part.

 Admitting that is a demotion, you have to accept it as **what can't be cured must be endured** as the depression is not over.

> 同義：忍得一時之氣，免得百日之憂
> Bottle up one's feelings.

> 反義：抵抗到底　To be dead set against.

tuì ér sī qí cì
退而思其次

If you cannot have the best, make the best of what you have.

If we can't as we would, we must do as we can.

Of two evils choose the least (lesser).

Better the devil you know than the devil you don't know.

 When money can not solve our problem, we **retreat and think about the second best**.

> **反義：**得寸進尺
> Give him an inch and he will take an ell.

zhēn fēng xiāng duì
針鋒相對
Give tit for tat.

Measure for measure.
A Roland for an Oliver.
Measure swords.

例句 ■■ He does not speak to me; so I **give tit for tat** to him by not even look at him.

出處 ■■ 景德傳燈錄："夫一切問答，如針鋒相投，無纖毫參差。"

> **同義：**以眼還眼，以牙還牙
> An eye for an eye; a tooth for a tooth.

> **反義：**互忍互讓　Live and let live.

十畫

fǔ dǐ chōu xīn

釜底抽薪

Take away fuel, take away flame (fire).

 Mark changed his subject to calm the angry crowd, **to take away fuel** is to **take away flame**.

 魏收 · 為侯景叛移梁朝文："抽薪止沸，剪草除根。"

> 反義：火上加油　Pour oil on the flame.

gāo bù kě pān

高不可攀

At the top of the ladder.

High up in the stirrups.
Could not be had.

 The boss is **at the top of the ladder** and he will not meet anyone at this hour.

 文選 · 陳琳 · 為曹洪與魏文帝書："紫帶為垣，高不可登。"

gāo zhěn wú yōu

高枕無憂

A good conscience is a soft pillow.

A quiet conscience sleeps in thunder.

例句 ■■ He relaxed as **a good conscience is a soft pillow** after he had paid the debt.

同義： 生平不作虧心事，半夜敲門也不驚
A clear conscience is a coat of mail.

反義： 坐立不安　Sit on a bag of fleas.

---

gāo shì kuò bù

高視闊步

Prance (swagger) about.

Give oneself airs.
Independent as a hog on ice.
Walk with one's nose in the air.

例句 ■■ John **pranced about** in his room in his robe.

出處 ■■ 魏文帝・漢文論："得闊步高談，無危懼之心。"

同義： 趾高氣揚　Ride the high horse.

反義： 作揖打拱　Bow and scrape.

十畫

gāo tán kuò lùn
高談闊論
To enlarge oneself.

To prate about.

 He loves **to enlarge himself** in talking about politics.

 元曲選 · 賈仲明 · 玉梳記："倚仗着高談闊論，全用些野狐涎撲子弟，打郎君。"

同義：談天說地　Talk of everything under the sun.
反義：欲說還休　To shut up shop.

guǐ guǐ suì suì
鬼鬼祟祟
Up to some hangky-pangky.

Up to some hangky-pangky.
Hole-and-corner.

 The boy sneaked out his room **up to some hangky-panky** late in the night.

同義：偷偷摸摸　On the sly.
反義：光明磊落　To be open and aboveboard.

jiǎ gōng jì sī

假公濟私

Practise jobbery.

Abuse one's power.

例句 ■■ To use the budget to cover one's own expenses is to **practice jobbery**.

出處 ■■ 元曲選．陳州糶米："他假公濟私，我怎肯和他干罷了也呵。"

同義：飽慳私囊　Line one's pocket.

成語故事：(There is) Nothing like leather

按字面直譯是"沒有像皮革那樣（好）的東西"。此語源於"伊索寓言"：某一城市被敵軍包圍，市民舉行會議討論如何防守，有個鞋匠站起來說道：Gentlemen... there's nothing in the world like leather。世界上最好的是皮革。寓言的寓意是說人們總認為自己的最好。做哪一行的總是說那一行最好，為自己的好處着想。類似的諺語有：Every man for his own trade，也就是我們的俗諺所說的："人不為己，天誅地滅"的意思。

yǎ kǒu wú yán
啞口無言
Come to a nonplus.

Be rendered speechless.

 Robert **came to a nonplus** when he was asked about his failure in the deal.

同義：瞠目結舌	Stare tongue-tied.
反義：滔滔不絕	Talk nine words at once.

wéi mìng shì cóng
唯命是從
Do as one is told.

A yes-man.
At one's beck and call.
Under the thumb of
To be at one's service.
To be in a person's pocket.
To come to heel.
Jump through a hoop.
Do something at the drop of the hat.

One can only **do as one is told** if it is one's supervisor who gives the order.

同義：百依百順　Dance after someone's pipe.

反義：我行我素　Take one's own course.

yín chī mǎo liáng

寅吃卯糧

Outrun the constable.

Live beyond one's means.

Live above one's income.

Who more than he is worth to spend, he maketh a rope his life to end.

 To expand the organisation with defficit still on is to **outrun the constable**.

同義：饔飧不繼
　　　　Can hardly make both ends meet.

反義：積穀防饑　Lay up against a rainy day.

zhuān xīn zhì zhì

專心致志

Set one's heart on

Devote oneself to
With undivided attention.
Wrapped up in

例句 ▪▪ You **set your heart on** what you are doing to ensure your success.

出處 ▪▪ 孟子‧告子上：" 不專心致志，則不得也。"

> 同義：兩耳不聞窗外事　Turn a deaf ear to

十一畫

jiāng jì jiù jì

將計就計

Turn to advantage an enemy's plot.

Beat someone at his own game.
Give Rowland for an Oliver.

例句 ▪▪ The best way to beat your enemy is to **turn to advantage an enemy's plot**.

> 同義：請君入甕
> Give a person his own medicine.

yōng rén zì rǎo
庸人自擾
Much ado about nothing.

Shearing of hogs.
The devil rides on a fiddlestick.
Borrow trouble.
Fret over nothing.

 To get into such trivialities is **much ado about nothing**.

 唐書 · 陸象先傳： "天下本無事，庸人自擾之。"

> **同義：** 自找麻煩 Invite trouble.

zhāng kǒu jié shé
張口結舌
To be tongue-tied.

Left speechless.
Lose one's tongue.
At a loss for words.
Gape with astonishment.

 George **is tongue-tied** when his wife asks where he was last night.

出處 晉·陸機·謝平原內史表：〝鉗口結舌，不敢上訴所天。〞

同義：無言可對　Come to a nonplus.
反義：口若懸河　Talk nine words at once.

zhāng yá wǔ zhǎo
張牙舞爪
Bare one's fangs.

Show one's claws (teeth).

例句 Don't **bare your fangs** to your comrade.

出處 敦煌變文集·孔子項托相問書：〝魚生二口游於江湖，龍生三日張牙舞爪。〞

同義：劍拔弩張　At daggers drawn.
反義：不露鋒芒　Draw in one's horns.

zhāng huáng shī cuò
張惶失措
Lose one's head.

At a loss what to do.

Scared out of one's wits.

 Jack **lost his head** in dealing with his strong opponent.

同義： 不知所措　Stand at gaze.
反義： 不慌不忙　At one's ease.

qiáng nǔ zhī mò
強弩之末
On its last legs.

Worn to a frazzle.
A spent arrow.
On the decline.

 Their business is **on its last legs** through bad management.

 漢書 · 韓安國傳：" 強弩之末，力不能入魯縞。"

同義： 大勢已去 Come out of the little end of the horn.
反義： 方興未艾　In the ascendant.

dé bù cháng shī

得不償失

The game is not worth the candle.

Give a lark to catch a kite.
Pay dear for the whistle.
More kicks than halfpence.

例句 ■■ You'll find **the game is not worth the candle** if you put your money on that horse.

出處 ■■ 蘇軾詩：〝感時嗟事變，所得不償失。〞

同義：以珠彈雀　Not worth powder and shot.
反義：一本萬利　Light gains make heavy purses.

dé xīn yìng shǒu

得心應手

As clay in the hands of the potter.

Get into one's stride.
Take to something like duck to water.

例句 ■■ For you to teach the primary school is **as clay in the hands of the potter**.

出處 ■■ 莊子‧天道：〝不徐不疾，得之於手而應於心。〞

> **反義：**心勞日拙　To be a fool for one's pains.

dé yì wàng xíng

得意忘形

Leap out of one's skin.

Beside oneself with joy.
Leap with joy.
To tread on air.
Turn one's head.

 He is ready to **leap out of his skin** on learning that he has been awarded the scholarship.

晉書・阮籍傳：「當其得意，忽忘形骸。」

> **同義：**手舞足蹈　Dance for joy.

dé yì yáng yáng

得意洋洋

Have one's nose (tail) in the air.

In high feather.
Feel one's oats.

Jack **has his nose in the air** after his promotion.

同義：洋洋自得　To tread on air.

反義：心灰意冷　To lose heart.

dé guò qiě guò
得過且過

Let well enough alone.

To muddle along.

 It's not easy to find a job, so **let well enough alone** with what you have now.

 陶宗儀·輟耕錄：〝寒號蟲至深冬嚴寒之際，自鳴日，得過且過。〞

同義：馬馬虎虎　Fair to middling.

反義：一絲不苟　Dot one's i's and cross one's t's.

cōng róng bú pò
從容不迫

Take things easy.

Take one's time.

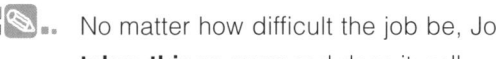
Cool as a cucumber.

例句 ▪▪ No matter how difficult the job be, John always **takes things easy** and does it well.

出處 ▪▪ 史記："良嘗聞從容步遊下邳圯上。"

同義：慢條斯理　Make two bites of a cherry.

反義：急不可待　Eat the calf in the cow's belly.

---

cóng shàn rú liú
從善如流

If the counsel be good, no matter who gave it.

例句 ▪▪ Jack does not like John, but he accepted his advice – **if the counsel be good, no matter who gave it**.

出處 ▪▪ 左傳："從善如流，宜哉。" / 國語："從善如登，從惡如崩。"

同義：三人行必有我師，擇其善者而從之
　　　Keep good men company and you shall be of the number.

huàn nàn zhī jiāo

患難之交

Foul weather friends.

A friend in need is a friend indeed.

 John and Jack went through many troubles together to become **foul weather friends**.

同義：風雨同舟　In the same boat.	
反義：酒肉朋友　Fair-weather friends.	

qíng bù zì jìn

情不自禁

Can't help

Emotion gets the better of oneself.
Feel an irresistible impulse.
Feel impelled to
Can't refrain from

 The movie is so touching that she **can't help** to shed tears.

wǎng rán ruò shī

惘然若失

Feel lost.

To be left up a tree.
To be all adrift.
To be at sea.

例句 Robert **felt lost** when he learned that he did not get the scholarship.

出處 後漢書 · 黃憲傳："同郡戴良,才高倨傲,而見憲未嘗不正容,及歸惘然若有失也。"

> **反義**:悠然自得 Free and easy.

jiē èr lián sān

接二連三

One after another.

In rapid succession.

例句 Visitors called on him **one after another**.

> **同義**:紛至沓來 Thick and fast.

jiē zhǒng ér zhì

接踵而至

Tread on the heels of

 John **treaded on the heels of** Jack to come to see me.

 戰國策·齊策："若隨踵而至也，今子一朝而見七士，則士不亦眾乎。"

同義：緊跟　Follow hard after
反義：姍姍來遲　Arrive in an armchair.

jié zú xiān dēng

捷足先登

Beat someone to it.

Beat someone to the draw.

 John **beats Jack to it** in getting the scholarship sponsored by the press.

 史記："蒯通曰，秦失其鹿，天下共逐之，高材捷足者先得焉。"

> **同義**：先到為君，後到為臣
> He that comes first to the hill may sit where
> he will.

> **反義**：姍姍來遲　Arrive in an armchair.

pěng fù dà xiào
捧腹大笑

Hold one's sides with laughter.

Convulsed with laughter.
Shake one's sides.

例句 Jack **holds his sides with laughter** while watching
that TV program.

出處 史記："司馬季主捧腹大笑。"

> **同義**：笑破肚皮　Split one's sides.

> **反義**：痛哭流涕　Break into a passion of tears.

diào yǐ qīng xīn

掉以輕心

Take it lightly.

Make light of
Lower one's guard.

例
句 ■■ It's an important job, you must not **take it lightly**.

出
處 ■■ 柳宗元 · 論師道書："故吾每為文章,未嘗敢以輕心
掉之。"

同義:毫不在意	To make nothing of
反義:嚴陣以待	Poised for action.

guà yáng tóu mài gǒu ròu

掛羊頭,賣狗肉

Cry up wine and sell vinegar.

例
句 ■■ He is **crying up wine and selling vinegar** by saying
that his new book is the best on that subject.

同義:以假亂真	Foist a thing off on one.

tuī sān zǔ sì

推三阻四

Make lame excuses.

A bad excuse is better than none.

例句 ■ Jack **makes lame excuses** to delay his payment.

出處 ■ 荊釵傳傳奇："恁推三阻四，莫不是行濁言清。"

> **反義**：勇挑重擔　Bite off a big chunk.

tuī jǐ jí rén

推己及人

Put oneself in another's shoes.

He that pities another remembers himself.

例句 ■ John always **puts himself in another's shoes** to treat people well.

出處 ■ 論語 · 顏淵："己所不欲，勿施於人。"

> **同義**：老吾老以及人之老　Charity begins at home.

> **反義**：人人為我　Every man for himself.

tuī xīn zhì fù

推心置腹

A heart to heart talk.

From the bottom of one's heart.
Take into confidence.
Let down one's hair.
Bare one's heart.

 The father has **a heart to heart talk** with his son about the boy's future.

 後漢書・光武帝紀上：＂蕭王推赤心置人腹中，安得不投死乎。＂

同義：促膝談心　Get knee to knee with one.
反義：諱莫如深　Keep one's own counsel.

十一畫

tuī bō zhù lán

推波助瀾

Pour oil on the fire.

Add fuel to the flame.
Fan the fire.
Egg someone on.

例句 ■■ Do not **pour oil on the fire** by telling the boss that we are in deficit when he has just lost money in the race.

出處 ■■ 文中子・問易：〝真君建德之事，適足推波助瀾，縱風止燎爾。〞

> **同義：**火上加油　Like a red rag to a bull.

> **反義：**息事寧人　Take the monkey off one's back.

shě jǐ wèi rén
捨己為人
To bell the cat.

例句 ■■ Jack volunteered **to bell the cat** and told the boss that he is to be blamed for the fault.

出處 ■■ 論語・先進・朱熹注：〝曾點之學……初無舍己為人之意。〞

> **反義：**假公濟私　To practise jobbery.

shě běn zhú mò
捨本逐末
Stick at trifles.

Kill the goose that lay the golden eggs.
Penny wise, pound foolish.

例句 ■■ Nothing can be accomplished if we **stick at trifles**, overlooking the whole situation.

出處 ■■ 晉書："農桑不修，遊食者多，皆由去本逐末故也。"

shě shēng qǔ yì
捨生取義
Die for a cause.

Die a martyr.
Lay down one's life.

例句 ■■ The revolutionist told the court that he would **die for the cause** of world peace.

出處 ■■ 孟子‧告子上："生，亦我所欲也，義，亦我所欲也，二者不可得兼，舍生而取義者也。"

同義：從容就義　Die a martyr's death.
反義：明哲保身　Be wordly wise and play safe.

jiù sǐ fú shāng

救死扶傷

Rescue the perishing.

Care for the dying.

例句 ■■ The team was sent there to **rescue the perishing** from the disaster.

出處 ■■ 司馬遷・報任少卿書："所殺過當,虜救死扶傷不 給。"

同義:扶危濟困 Help a lame dog over a stile.
反義:荼毒生靈 Mow down like grass.

jiào xué xiāng zhǎng

教學相長

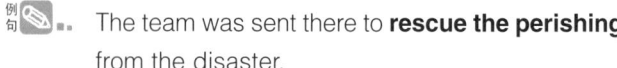

Teaching others teaches one's self.

例句 ■■ She wishes to be a teacher, believing that **teaching others teaches herself as well**.

出處 ■■ 禮記・學記："學然後知不足,教然後知困。知不足 然後能自反也,知困然後能自強也,故曰教學相長 也。"

wàng yáng xīng tàn

望洋興歎

Feel helpless and powerless.

The fish that we did not catch is a very large one.
Distance lends enchantment to the view.

 One has to try one's best instead of sitting there and **feeling helpless and powerless**.

 莊子·秋水："於是焉，河伯始旋其面目，望洋向若而歎。"

> **同義**：臨淵羨魚不如退而結網
> The end of fishing is not angling but catching.

wàng yǎn yù chuān

望眼欲穿

Look forward to

Hanker after
All agog.

 George is **looking forward to** a reply to his application letter.

 白居易·寄微之詩："白頭吟處變，青眼望中穿。"

> **同義：**望穿秋水 Hope against hope.

wàng chén mò jí
望塵莫及
Not fit to hold a candle to one.

To be nowhere.

例句 ■ Speaking of achievement, Jack is **not fit to hold a candle to James**.

出處 ■ 南史："吳不解而退，琨追謝之，望塵不及矣。"

> **同義：**瞠乎其後 Lag far behind.

> **反義：**遙遙領先 Streets ahead of

hùn shuǐ mō yú
混水摸魚
Take advantage of

To fish in troubled waters.

例句 ■ The congressman **took advantage of** the confrontation of parties to get himself selected to the committee.

> **同義：**鷸蚌相持，漁人得利
>
> Two dogs fight for a bone, and a third runs away with it.

shēn jū jiǎn chū
深居簡出
Live in seclusion.

Like a hermit.
Keep oneself to oneself.

例句 ▪ Tom **lives in seclusion** after his retirement.

出處 ▪ 秦觀・謝王學士書：“深居簡出，幾不與世人相通。”

> **同義：**息交絕遊　Retire into oneself.
>
> **反義：**拋頭露面　Come out into the open.

tián yán mì yǔ
甜言蜜語
Give one a mouthful of moonshine.

Pretty lies.
Fine-sounding words.

例句 ■ Jack **gave his girlfriend a mouthful of moonshine**, promissing to buy a diamond ring as birthday gift for her.

出處 ■ 宵光劍傳奇：「甜言蜜語三冬煖，血污遊魂萬里沙。」

yì kǒu tóng shēng
異口同聲
Be of one voice.

With one accord.
In chorus.

例句 ■ All her students **are in one voice**, saying that she is the best teacher in their college.

出處 ■ 宋書 · 庾炳之傳：「今之事跡，異口同音。」

> **反義**：莫衷一是 Agree like the clocks of London.

yì xiǎng tiān kāi
異想天開
Cry for the moon.

Have one's head full of bees.
Flight of fancy.

Wishful thinking.
Farfetched.

 To ask for a contribution to the rescue fund from that miser is to **cry for the moon**.

同義：想入非非　Build castles in the air.

反義：實事求是　Look fact in the face.

十
一
畫

shèng qì líng rén
盛氣凌人
To lift up the horn.

Throw one's weight about.
To be overbearing.

 With his boss at his side, Jack **lifts up the horn** in dealing with us.

 戰國策："左師觸龍言願見太后，太后盛氣而胥之。"

同義：仗勢欺人　Pull rank on someone.

反義：和藹可親　Easy to get along with.

zhòng mù kuí kuí
眾目睽睽

There is a witness everywhere.

例句 ■■ **There is witness everywhere** to the fact that he is innocent.

出處 ■■ 韓愈："萬目睽睽。"

> **同義：**有目共睹　One would be blind not to see.

> **反義：**神不知，鬼不覺　On the sly.

zhòng zhì chéng chéng
眾志成城

Union (unity) is strength.

Make a united effort.

例句 ■■ Let's carry our plan out together－**union is strength**.

出處 ■■ 國語・周語下："眾心成城，眾口鑠金。"

> **反義：**獨木不成林　One flower makes no garland.

成語故事：Union is strength

團結就是力量，這個常見人用的格言，據說是古希臘時代的諺語。希臘詩聖荷馬（Homer）在史詩"伊利亞特"中有：Union gives strength, even to weak men。（即使弱者，亦因團結而得到力量。）名句，即以古諺為據。伊索寓言中亦有：Union gives strength 之語。培根（Francis Bacon）有"力量因團結而更強"（Strength united is the greater）之語。富蘭克林（Benjamin Franklin，1844-1924）在獨立宣言中也說過。

yǎn zhōng dīng

眼中釘

A thorn in the eye.

An eyesore.

例句 ■■ That old woman hates George very much and takes him as **a thorn in the eye**.

出處 ■■ 馮贄・雲仙雜記："趙在禮在宋州所為不法……一日制下，移鎮永興，百姓相賀曰，眼中釘拔卻矣。"

同義：肉中刺　A pain in the neck.

反義：掌上明珠　The apple of one's eye.

xí yǐ wéi cháng

習以為常

Get into the way of

Get into one's stride.
An old dog cannot alter his way of barking.
Custom reconciles us to everything.
Get used to it as a skinned eel.

例句 ■■ I go to bed at ten every night, **getting into the way of** my life.

出處 ■■ 宋·釋道原·景德傳燈錄："鄉洞獠民畏鬼神，多淫祀，殺牛釃酒，習以為常。"

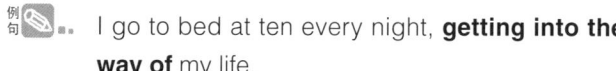

成語故事：Habit is a second nature

　　按字面譯，該是"習慣是第二天性"，但我們一般譯作"習慣成自然"。這諺語出典於古羅馬政治家西塞羅 (Marcus Tullius Cicero，公元前 106-43) 的論結局 (De Finibus，即 On Ends) 文中。拉丁原文 Consuetudine quasi altaram quadam naturam effici 之英譯：Custom produce a kind of second nature。莎士比亞在"王子復仇記" (Hamlet) 一劇第三幕第四場中引用作：For use almost can change the stamp of nature.

tuō yǐng ér chū

脫穎而出

Hit the head-line.

To be head and shoulders taller.

 John **hit the headline** after the publication of his novel.

 史記 · 平原君虞卿列傳： "使遂早得處囊中，乃脫穎而出。"

同義：出人頭地 Come to the fore.
反義：平平庸庸 Pass in a crowd in a push.

mò míng qí miào

莫名其妙

Past comprehension.

To be at sea.
It's neither rhyme nor reason.
Can make neither head nor tail of

 His poor excuse is nothing but a **past comprehension**.

同義：莫測高深 To be out of one's depth.

十一畫

mò nì zhī jiāo
莫逆之交
A sworn friend.

Get along well with each other.
A bosom friend.

 John is **a sworn friend** of Jack whom he knows for years.

 莊子・大宗師："三人相視而笑，莫逆於心，遂相與為友。"

同義：管鮑之誼　Damon and Pythias.
反義：不共戴天之仇　Deadly feud.

chǔ xīn jī lù
處心積慮
After long deliberation.

By design.

 He carried out his plot **after long deliberation**, thinking little about others.

 穀梁傳："何甚乎鄭伯，甚鄭伯之處心積慮成於殺也。"

同義：深思熟慮	Turn is over in one's mind.
反義：心血來潮	On the impulse of the moment.

xiù shǒu páng guān
袖手旁觀
Stand by (Look on) with folded arms.

Stand aloof.
Sitting on the fence.
Leave one to sink or swim.

例句 ■■ We can't **stand by with folded arms** when we see so many people suffering from the Tsunami.

出處 ■■ 韓愈・祭柳子厚文："巧匠旁觀，縮手袖間。"

同義：冷眼旁觀	To be outside the ropes.
反義：全力以赴	Put one's shoulder to the wheel.

shè shēn chǔ dì
設身處地
To be in someone else's shoes.

Put oneself in the place of others.

Put oneself in another's shoes.

 One should **be in his contender's shoes** in order to get a whole picture of the problem.

 禮記・中庸："體羣臣也。"朱熹注："體謂設以身，處其地而察以心也。"

zé wú páng dài
責無旁貸

Can't pass the buck.

To be duty-bound.
With bounden duty.

 The job is yours and you **can't pass the buck** to me.

 詩經："靡不有初，鮮克有終。"

同義：義不容辭　Make a virtue of necessity.
反義：事不關己，高高掛起 It's none of my business.

tān dé wú yàn

貪得無饜

One's greed cannot be satisfied.

As greedy as a wolf.

 Jack always asks for more money as **his greed cannot be satisfied**.

左傳・昭二十八年："貪婪無饜。"

> **同義**：我的就是我的，你的也是我的
> Heads I win, tails you lose.

> **反義**：知足常足
> A contented mind is a perpetual feast.

十一畫

tān zāng wǎng fǎ

貪贓枉法

Line one's purse (pocket).

Feather one's nest.

 The corrupted official **lines his purse**, accepting bribes as gifts.

同義：貪污腐化	Have an itching palm.
反義：廉潔清正	Have clean hands.

成語故事：Do not put new wine into old bottles

勿將新酒裝入舊瓶中，和我們説的 "舊瓶裝新酒" 似乎都是俗諺，其實不然。這句成語典於聖經新約馬太福音第九章第十七節（也沒有人將新酒裝在舊皮袋裏。若是這樣，皮袋就裂開，酒漏出來，連皮袋也壞了。）從前以山羊皮作的袋裝酒，old bottle 是這種酒袋，故中譯聖經此段中作酒袋。愛喝白蘭地酒的朋友説名酒之瓶被小人用來裝劣酒，如此的舊瓶裝劣酒，成了生財之道，可嘆，可悲者也。

zhǐ gāo qì yáng

趾高氣揚

In high snuff.

Ride the high horse.

Give oneself airs.

To strut about.

Hoity-toity.

例句 ■■ Jack deals with friends **in high snuff** after his promotion.

出處 ■■ 左傳・桓十三年：「莫敖必敗，舉趾高，心不固矣。」

同義：高視闊步　Prance about.

反義：垂頭喪氣　Hang one's head.

xiāo yáo zì zài
逍遙自在
To be carefree.

Free and easy.

例句 ■■ He retired and feels **to be carefree** to enjoy life.

出處 ■■ 五燈會元：「二十四臘，逍遙自在，逢人則喜，見佛不拜。」

同義：優哉悠哉　At one's ease.

反義：疲於奔命　Run off one's feet.

tōng xiāo dá dàn

通宵達旦

All night long.

From dusk to dawn.
All through the night.
The whole night through.
Round-the-clock.

 They played poker **all night long**.

sù zhàn sù jué

速戰速決

Get it over and done with.

He that runs fast will not run long.
Blitz tactics.
Make short work of
Launch a blitzkrieg.

 Let's pull together to **get it over and done with**.

反義：穩紮穩打　Slow but sure wins the race.

yě xīn bó bó
野心勃勃
Ruthlessly ambitious.

To level at the moon.
To fly at high game.
The sky is one's limit.
Burn with ambition.
Hitch one's wagon to a star.

 The man is **ruthlessly ambitions** as it is known that he has written to the president a letter on world peace.

> 反義：當一天和尚撞一天鐘
> Come day, go day, God send Sunday.

chén cí làn diào
陳詞濫調
Hackneyed phrases.

Flog the dead horse.
Harp on the same string.

 The official statement is full of **hackneyed phrases**.

xuě shàng jiā shuāng
雪上加霜

Troubles never come singly.

One misfortune comes on the neck of another.

 The poor widow lost her investment in that bankrupt shop, **troubles never come singly**.

 景德傳燈錄："伊禪謂大陽和尚雪上更加霜。"

> **同義：**禍不單行　It never rains but it pours.

xuě zhōng sòng tàn
雪中送炭

A friend in need is a friend indeed.

Help a lame dog over a stile.

 George knew that I am in debt and loan me some money; **a friend in need is a friend indeed**.

 宋 · 范成大 · 大雪送炭與芥隱詩："不是雪中須送炭，聊裝風景要詩來。"

shèng bǐ yì chóu

勝彼一籌

One stroke above.

Pip someone at the post.
Have an edge on one.
One too many for a person.
Take the wind out of one's sails.
Go somebody one better.

例句 John is **one stroke above** Jack in the contest.

同義：棋高一着　To be one up on a person.
反義：相形見絀　Pale beside another.

十
二
畫

bó xué duō cái

博學多才

Know a thing or two.

Know what's what.
Well-read.

例句 Believe me, he **knows a thing or two**.

同義：多才多藝　To be all-round.
反義：胸無點墨　Not to know A from a windmill.

tí xiào jiē fēi

啼笑皆非

Laugh on the wrong side of one's mouth.

What a cheek!

 They were made to **laugh on the wrong side of their mouths** by an unforeseen occurrence.

 陳 · 樂昌公主 · 餞別自解："笑啼俱不敢，方信為人難。"

xǐ chū wàng wài

喜出望外

Go into rapture.

Beyond expectation.
To one's pleasant surprise.
Get more than one bargained for
To be overjoyed.

 The girl **went into rapture** when she got the job.

 蘇軾 · 與李之儀書："辱書尤數，喜出望外。"

> **同義：**乞漿得酒
>   Fish for sprats and catch a herring.

xǐ xíng yú sè

喜形於色

Put on a smiling face.

Radiant with joy.
A merry heart makes a cheerful countenance.

例句 ■■ She **puts on a smiling face** on hearing the good news.

出處 ■■ 宋‧孫光憲‧北夢瑣言：“見其喜形於色，駐馬懇詰。”

反義：愁眉苦臉　Pull a long face.

xǐ nù wú cháng

喜怒無常

Go into hysterics.

例句 ■■ The stroke made the poor man to **go into hysterics** in his daily life.

出處 ■■ 呂氏春秋：“喜怒無處，言談日易。”

> 同義：東邊日出西邊雨
> The devil is beating his wife with a shoulder of mutton.

> 反義：不動聲色　Keep a straight face.

xǐ qì yáng yáng
喜氣洋洋
Beam with joy.

Light up with pleasure.

例句 ✍ ▪▪ John was **beaming with joy** after his engagement with Jean had been announced.

> 同義：其樂融融　Merry as a cricket.

> 反義：怒氣沖沖　Vent one's anger.

xún xù jiàn jìn
循序漸進
Step by step.

Advance by small degrees.

Inch forward.

By stages.

例句 ■. The operation has to be carried out **step by step**.

出處 ■. 語出《論語·憲問·朱熹注》

> **同義**：由淺入深　Learn to walk before you run.

> **反義**：僭隊　Jump the queue.

xún guī dǎo jǔ

循規蹈矩

Toe the line (mark).

Walk the chalk.

Follow the beaten track.

例句 ■. Members of the party are told to **toe the line** set by the party.

出處 ■. 紅樓夢："看的你們是三四代老媽媽，最是循規蹈矩。"

> **反義**：無法無天　Lawless as a town-bull.

cè yǐn zhī xīn
惻隱之心
Milk of human kindness.

Bowels of compassion (mercy).
Sense of pity.

例句 ■ John contributed much to the Tsunami sufferers, he has the **milk of human kindness**.

出處 ■ 孟子："惻隱之心,人皆有之。"

> **反義**:嗜殺成性　To be blood thirsty.

huáng kǒng bù ān
惶恐不安
With one's heart going pit-pat.

例句 ■ Working with the boss in the same office room is to work **with one's heart going pit-pat**.

出處 ■ 漢書・王莽傳："人民正營,顏師古注,正營,惶恐不安也。"

> **反義**:心安理得　Have an easy conscience.

zhǎng shàng míng zhū
掌上明珠

Set on the pedestal.

The apple of one's eyes.

 The girl is **set on the pedestal** by her doting grandfather.

晉．傅玄．短歌行："昔君視我，如掌中珠，何意一朝，棄我溝渠。"

> **反義：**眼中釘　A thorn in the eye.

tí xīn diào dǎn
提心吊膽

To pull up one's socks.

Have one's heart in one's mouth.
In a blue funk.
On pins and needles.
On tenterhooks.

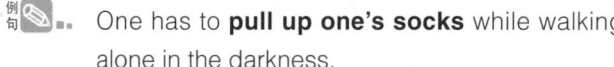 One has to **pull up one's socks** while walking alone in the darkness.

同義：七上八下　Drop off the hook.

反義：平生不作虧心事，半夜敲門也不驚
　　　　A quiet conscience sleeps in thunder.

---

huī jīn rú tǔ
揮金如土
Spend money like water.

Play ducks and drakes with one's money.
Throw money about.

 One must not **spend money like water** even one
　　　　has hit the jack pot.

同義：恣意揮霍　Money burns a hole in his pocket.

反義：守財奴　As tight as a drum.

---

yáng cháng ér qù
揚長而去
To light out.

Take a powder.

Make oneself scarce.
Fly the coop.
To beat it.

 He **light out** for the office the moment he hung up the phone.

同義：掉頭不顧　Never to look back.
反義：突如其來　Appear from nowhere.

qíng tiān pī lì
晴天霹靂
Catch one off guard.

A bolt from the blue.
It came absolutely out of the blue.
Out of the clear blue sky.

 The bad news **caught him off guard**.

 陸游詩："正如久蟄龍，青天飛霹靂。"

同義：突如其來　Appear from nowhere.

zhāo lìng xī gǎi
朝令夕改

The law is not the same at morning and night.

 The boss changed his mind and gave us his new order; **the law is not the same at morning and night**.

 漢書‧食貨志上：「急政暴虐，賦斂不時，朝令而夕改。」

同義：出爾反爾　Go back on one's word.
反義：貫徹始終　Carry through to the end.

zhāo qì péng bó
朝氣蓬勃

Brim over with high spirit.

Fresh as a daisy.
Full of vigour and vitality.
Look as if one has come out of a bandbox.

 The boy, **brimmed over with high spirit**, joined his father to fish.

 孫子‧軍事：「是故朝氣銳，晝氣惰，暮氣歸。」

同義：英姿煥發　In one's vigorous youth.

反義：暮氣沉沉　Lose one's grip.

zhāo qín mù chǔ
朝秦暮楚

In a switch of loyalties.

Play fast and loose.
Blow hot and cold.

例句 ▪▪ Jack, **in a switch of loyalties**, resigned and joined another firm.

出處 ▪▪ 宋・晁補之・北渚亭賦：「托生理於四方，固朝秦而暮楚。」

反義：忠心耿耿　As true as the dial to the sun.

yóu shǒu hào xián
游手好閒

Keep one's hands in one's pockets.

Lounge around.
Fool away one's time.

Do a mike.

例句 .. Do something productive, don't **keep your hands in your pocket**.

出處 .. 晉書："鄉無游手，邑不廢時。"

同義：吊兒郎當　Gad about.
反義：事務紛繁　Up to the ears in work.

wú zhōng shēng yǒu
無中生有
A pure invention.

Sheer fabrication.
Made out of thin air.

例句 .. What people said about John is **a pure invention**.

出處 .. 老子："天下萬物生於有，有生於無。"

同義：向壁虛構　Trump up a story.
反義：鐵證如山　Iron-clad evidence.

成語故事：Nothing comes from nothing

一般譯作"無中不生有"，是源於古希臘的格言。伊壁鳩魯（Epicurus，公元前 341-270）的哲學觀點，也是物理學的理論基礎。拉丁語作：Nihil ex nihilo fit，據說是喬叟英譯之作。莎士比亞在"李爾王"（King Lear）中曾引用之（考地莉亞和李爾的對話中後者説：Nothing will come of nothing, speak again。）此語又作：Nothing for nothing，又譯作"有來有去"，並非"有求必應"。求神還要燒香，世界上似乎都要有來有去。

wú suǒ bù wéi
無所不為
Go to any limit.

Up to every evil.
Stop at nothing.

例句 ■■ To make ends meet, he will **go to any limit** to earn more money.

出處 ■■ 三國志‧吳志‧張溫傳："揆其奸心，無所不為。"

同義：作惡多端	Up to all sorts of evils.
反義：安分守己	Know one's distance.

wú suǒ shì shì
無所事事
At a loose end.

Twiddle one's thumbs.

 Jack has been **at loose ends** ever since he lost his job.

同義：閒暇無事	Kick one's heel.
反義：忙忙碌碌	As busy as a bee.

wú suǒ shì cóng
無所適從
Torn between.

At a loss what to do.

Not knowing which way to turn.

例句 ■ John is **torn between** two offers from two big firms.

出處 ■ 宋 · 姚寬 · 西溪叢語："源殊派異，無所適從。"

同義：惘然若失 Feel lost.
反義：心中有數 Know one's own mind.

wú bìng shēn yín
無病呻吟
Full of grumbles.

Cry out before one is hurt.
The sea complains it wants water.
Make a fuss about nothing.

例句 ■ He is always **full of grumbles** about being ill although he is quite strong.

出處 ■ 宋 · 辛棄疾 · 臨江仙詞："更歡須歎息，無病也呻吟。"

反義：臨難不懼 Look death in the face.

wú lǐ qǔ nào
無理取鬧
Make a scene.

Pick up a quarrel with
Find fault with a fat goose.
To fly in the face of

例句 ■■ Every time he gets drunk he **makes a scene**.

出處 ■■ 韓愈・答柳柳州食蝦蟆詩："鳴聲相呼和，無理只取
鬧。"

> **反義**：以理服人　Bring one to reason.

wú wēi bú zhì
無微不至
Show every concern.

Wait on one hand and foot.

例句 ■■ She **shows every concern** for the welfare of her
clients.

> **同義**：大獻殷勤　Dance attendance on

> **反義**：要理不理　Leave one in the cold.

wú xiè kě jī

無懈可擊

Have no fault to find with

例句 ▪▪ The people **have no fault to find with** the new government.

出處 ▪▪ 孫子・曹操注：「擊其懈怠，出其空虛。」

同義：完美無缺　The pink of perfection.
反義：破綻百出　Show the cloven foot.

yóu yí bù jué

猶疑不決

To be capricious.

Like one o'clock half struck.
Between hawk and buzzard.
To shilly-shally.
In two minds about something.

例句 ▪▪ He **is capricious** about whether he should take the job.

出處 ▪▪ 戰國策・趙策：「平原君猶豫未有所決。」

> **同義：**優柔寡斷　To be neither off nor on.

> **反義：**快刀斬亂麻　Cut the Gordian knot.

huà shé tiān zú
畫蛇添足
Gild refined gold.

Paint the lily.

例句 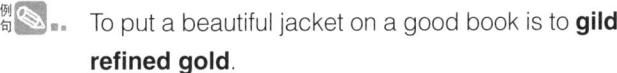 To put a beautiful jacket on a good book is to **gild refined gold**.

出處 戰國策：「畫地為蛇，先成者飲，一人蛇先成，引酒，且言吾能為之足，未成，一人蛇成，奪其巵。」

> **同義：**多此一舉　Carry water to the river.

tòng gǎi qián fēi
痛改前非
Make a fresh start.

Turn over a new leaf.
Mend one's way.

He was on probation and **made a fresh start** by working for the welfare of the public.

同義：重新做人　Start with a clean slate.
反義：堅決不改　To sit tight.

fā rén shēn xǐng
發人深省
Set one to thinking.

Provide food for thought.
Give one something to think about.

 His failure **set him to thinking** about the limits of human resources.

杜甫詩："欲覺聞晨鐘，令人發深省。"

fā hào shī lìng
發號施令
Lay down the law.

Call the tune.

The ruler **laid down the law** that common people could not own pistols.

 尚書 · 冏命：「發號施令，罔有不臧。」

同義：指手劃腳　To lord it over.
反義：唯命是從　Do one's bidding.

jīn pí lì jié
筋疲力竭
Dog-tired.

To be worn (played, pumped) out.
To be dead beat.
More dead than alive.
Ready to drop.
Dead on one's feet.
Worn to a frazzle.

 Jack felt **dog-tired** after the tennis match.

同義：疲於奔命　To be dead tired.
反義：精力旺盛　Full of beans.

jiǎo jìn nǎo zhī

絞盡腦汁

To rack one's brain.

Cudgel (rack) one's brain.

 John **racked his brain** to figure out the meaning of the letter.

同義：搜索枯腸　Beat one's brain out.

反義：飽食終日，無所用心
A belly full of gluttony will never study willingly.

十二畫

xù xù bù xiū

絮絮不休

Talk the bark off a tree.

Hold a person by the button.
To hold forth.

 Whenever she talk about her son, she **talk the bark off a tree**.

 兩抄摘腴："休休絮絮，我自明朝歸去。"

同義：話匣子　A chatter-box.

反義：三緘其口　Button up one's lip.

luò yì bù jué
絡繹不絕
In rapid succession.

An endless flow.
To be alive with

 Donations came in **in rapid succession** after the Tsunami disaster.

後漢書・東海恭王強傳："數遣使者太醫令丞，方使道術，絡繹不絕。"

同義：川流不息　A constant flow.

shàn shǐ shàn zhōng
善始善終
A good beginning makes a good ending.

Good to begin well, better to end well.
See a thing through.

例句 ■■ Let's keep on doing our best to finish the job as **a good beginning makes a good ending**.

出處 ■■ 莊子‧大宗師：" 善妖善老，善始善終，人猶效之。"

> **同義**：貫徹始終　Such beginning, such end.

píng shuǐ xiāng féng

萍水相逢

Merry meet, merry part.

Strike up an acquaintance with

例句 ■■ Jack and Jill, **merry meet, merry part**, became good friends.

出處 ■■ 王勃： " 萍水相逢，盡是他鄉之客。"

> **反義**：過訪不遇　Kiss the post.

xū yǒu qí biǎo

虛有其表

More poke than pudding.

A stuff shirt.
All is not gold that glitters.

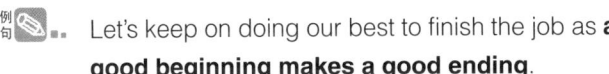

十二畫

More sauce than pig.

More squeak than wool.

A camouflage.

 Pay no attention to that guy's arrogance, he's **more poke than pudding**.

 鄭處誨 · 明皇雜錄 : "嵩既退,上擲其草於地曰,虛有其表耳。"

> **同義** : 金玉其外,敗絮其中
> Whited sepulchres, which indeed appear beautiful outward, but are within full of dead man's bones.

> **反義** : 名副其實　To be worthy of the name.

xū zhāng shēng shì

虛張聲勢

Barking dogs seldom bite.

His bark is worse than his bite.

Empty vessels make the most noise.

Show a bold front.

Cut a fat hog.
Be swashbuckling.

例句 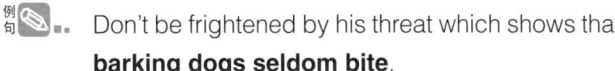 Don't be frightened by his threat which shows that **barking dogs seldom bite**.

出處 韓愈‧論淮西事宜狀：“然皆暗弱，自保無暇，虛張聲勢，則必有之。”

> **反義：**不動聲色　Set one's face like a flint.

píng tóu pǐn zú
評頭品足
Size one up.

Look a person up and down.
Pick one to pieces.
Try to find fault with

例句 The editorial **sized the new chairman up** with his past achievements.

出處 元史：“平居未嘗評品人物。”

> **同義：**吹毛求疵　Pick a hole in one's coat.

yí xiào dà fāng

貽笑大方

Expose oneself to ridicule.

Make an ass of oneself.
Cut a sorry figure.
Make a laughing stock of oneself.

 Don't **expose yourself to ridicule** by publishing your article on this subject.

 莊子・秋水： "吾長見笑於大方之家。"

> **同義：**有失體統　Drop a brick.

jìn tuì liǎng nán

進退兩難

In a dilemma.

Between the devil and the deep sea.
Get into a nice hobble.

 George is **in a dilemma** when he is asked to give a speech on his achievements.

 詩經： "人亦有言，進退維谷。"

> **同義：**進退維谷　On the horns of a dilemma.

liàng lì ér xíng

量力而行

Undertake no more than you can perform.

Raise no more spirits than you can conjure down.
Kindle not a fire that you cannot extinguish.

 To do a good job, you should **undertake no more than you can perform**.

 左傳・昭十年："力能則進，否則退，量力而行。"

> **反義**：自不量力　Bite off more than one can chew.

kāi juàn yǒu yì

開卷有益

A book that is shut is but a block.

Ask counsel of the dead.

 Reading makes a full man and **a book that is shut is but a block**.

 宋實錄："朕性喜讀書，頗得其趣，開卷有益，豈徒然也。"

> **反義**：盡信書不如無書
> Better untaught than ill taught.

kāi mén jiàn shān
開門見山

Come straight to the point.

Mince no matters.
Point-blank.

 He **came straight to the point**, saying that he is against our proposal.

 嚴羽 · 滄浪詩話 · 詩評：「太白發句，謂之開門見山。」

> **同義**：直言不諱　Without reserve.

> **反義**：閃爍其詞
> Speak with one's tongue in one's cheek.

kāi chéng bù gōng
開誠佈公

Wear one's heart on one's sleeve.

Put one's cards on the table.
Come into the open.

 People may take advantage of you if you always **wear your heart on your sleeve** in dealing with them.

出處 ■ 三國志‧蜀志‧諸葛亮傳評："諸葛亮之為相國也，
開誠心，佈公道。"

> **反義**：秘而不宣　Keep one's own counsel.

jí sī guǎng yì
集思廣益
Two heads are better than one.

Lay our heads together.
In the multitude of counsellors there is safety.

例句 ■ I am for brainstorming, **two heads are better than
one**.

出處 ■ 諸葛丞相集："夫參署者，集眾思廣忠益也。"

> **同義**：一人計短，二人計長
> Four eyes see more than two.
>
> **反義**：獨斷獨行　Take the law into one's own hand.

jí yè chéng qiú
集腋成裘
Many a mickle makes a muckle.

Little by little the bird builds its nest.

Little and often fills the purse.

例句 ■. The rescue fund comes to billions as **many a mickle makes a muckle**.

出處 ■. 慎子·知忠："狐白之裘，非一腋之皮也。"

> **同義**：涓滴成河　Every little helps.

shùn shǒu qiān yáng
順手牽羊
Make (Walk) away with

Walk (Make) off with

例句 ■. Someone **made away with** my billfold when I was in the bath.

> **同義**：不問自取　To make free with something.

hēi bái fēn míng
黑白分明
As plain as the nose on one's face.

The fairer the paper, the fouler the blot.
In sharp contrast.

例句 ■■ The fact is **as plain as the nose on one's face**, no more arguement is necessary.

出處 ■■ 春秋繁露：「黑白分明，然後民知所去就。」

luàn qī bā zāo
亂七八糟
All in a huddle.

At sixes and sevens.
Higgledy-piggledy.
A pretty kettle of fish.

例句 ■■ The room is **all in a huddle**.

同義：一塌糊塗　A devil of a mess.
反義：有條不紊　In apple-pie order.

qīng pén dà yǔ
傾盆大雨
To rain cats and dogs.

To rain trams and omnibuses.
Rain buckets.

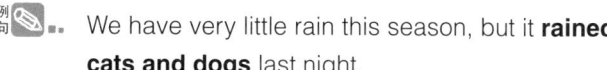

例句 ◾◾ We have very little rain this season, but it **rained cats and dogs** last night.

出處 ◾◾ 宋伯仁 · 雨中詩： "終日翻盆雨，池亭晚更涼。"

shì bù liǎng lì
勢不兩立
Opposite as fire and water.

At daggers drawn.
Would not touch one with a barge pole (a pair of tongs).

例句 ◾◾ They are **opposite as fire and water** in the campaign for chairmanship.

出處 ◾◾ 三國志 · 周瑜傳： "孤與老賊，勢不兩立。"

同義：不共戴天之仇　Inveterate enemy.
反義：通力合作　To pull together.

shì rú pò zhú
勢如破竹
Like slicing cheese.

Sweep everything before one.

It was just a walk over.
Bowl over like ninepins.
To win in a canter.
Like a hot knife cutting through butter.
Win in a breeze.

例句 ■ The victorious army advanced **like slicing cheese** and occupied the city.

出處 ■ 晉書‧杜預傳：“今兵威已振，譬如破竹，數節之後，皆迎刃而解。”

| **同義**：秋風掃落葉　Make a clean sweep. |
| **反義**：到處碰壁　Driven from pillar to post. |

十三畫

sài wēng shī mǎ　yān zhī fēi fú

塞翁失馬，焉知非福

A blessing in disguise.

Sometimes the best gain is to lose.
Sweet are the uses of adversity.

例句 ■ The doctor says that my broken leg should be looked on as **a blessing in disguise** since it will force me to take a long needed rest.

出處 ■ 淮南子："塞上叟失馬，人皆弔之，叟曰，此何詎不為福。"

> **同義：**禍為福所倚　Every cloud has a silver lining.

wēi bù zú dào
微不足道
Nothing to speak of

Not worth mentioning.
To be off the map.

例句 ■ My gift is **nothing to speak of**, just a token of respect.

> **同義：**不值一提　Nothing to make a song about.

> **反義：**碩大無朋　Look as big as bull beef.

yú mèi wú zhī
愚昧無知
Simple minded.

Not to know a hawk from a handsaw.
Not to know A from a windmill.

He is so **simple minded** that he does not know the whereabout of Beijing.

同義：目不識丁　Not to know B from a bull's foot.
反義：博學多才　Know what's what.

gǎn rén fèi fǔ

感人肺腑

Come home to one's heart.

Tug at one's heart strings.

 The story **came home to the girl's heart** and she weeped.

同義：扣人心弦　Pluck at one's heartstrings.

十三畫

xiǎng rù fēi fēi

想入非非

Imagine things.

Build castles in the air (Spain).
Have a bee in one's bonnet.
Go off into wild flights of fancy.
To be in the clouds.

Show him an egg, and instantly the whole air is full of feathers.

 Robert's idealistic view is his **imagined things**.

 楞嚴經："如存不存,若盡不盡,如是一類,名非想非非想處。"

> **同義**:異想天開　Cry for the moon.

> **反義**:腳踏實地　Come down to bedrock.

ài wū jí wū
愛屋及烏

Love me, love my dog.

He that loves the tree loves the branch.

 Jack walked Jill's dog every day, that's really: **Love me, love my dog**.

 説苑:"臣聞愛其人者,兼愛及屋上之烏。"

> **同義**:幼吾幼以及人之幼　Charity begins at home.

chóu méi kǔ liǎn

愁眉苦臉

Wear a glum countenance.

Laugh on the other side of one's face.
Pull a long face.

 The boy **wears a glum countenance** while listening to his teacher's lesson.

同義：哭喪着臉　To sour one's cheeks.
反義：笑容可掬　A face wreathed in smiles.

十三畫

yáo wěi qǐ lián

搖尾乞憐

Play up to

Curry favour with
Grovel in the dust.
Grovel at the feet of

 The woman **plays up to** that rich man, really disgraceful.

韓愈："若俛首帖耳，搖尾乞憐者，非我之志也。"

> **反義：**不屑一顧　Snap one's fingers at

yáo yáo yù zhuì
搖搖欲墜

Hang by a thread.

Hang on by one's eyelids (eyelashes).
Tremble in the balance.

例句 ▪ According to the physician in charge, his life is **hanging by a thread**.

出處 ▪ 淮南子・兵略訓："推其搖搖。"

> **同義：**危在旦夕　Sword of Damocles.

> **反義：**巋然屹立　Stand rock-firm.

jìng ér yuǎn zhī
敬而遠之

Keep one at a respectable distance.

The best remedy against an ill man is much ground between.
Prefer a person's room to his company.

Keep one at arm's length.
Give a wide berth to

例句 :: Robert is not very honest and we always **keep him at a respectable distance**.

出處 :: 論語‧雍也："敬鬼神而遠之。"

同義：避之則吉 Steer clear of
反義：依依不捨 Can't tear onself away.

tāo tāo bù jué
滔滔不絕

Talk oneself out of breath.

Talk nine words at once.
Talk a donkey's hind leg off.
Rattle off.
To talk against time.

例句 :: When Jack is lecturing, he always **talks himself out of breath**.

出處 :: 王仁裕‧開元天寶遺事："張九齡善談論，每與賓客議論經旨，滔滔不竭，如下阪走丸也。"

十三畫

同義：絮絮不休	To hold forth.
反義：張口結舌	To be tongue-tied.

huàn rán yī xīn
煥然一新
Look spick and span.

Take on a new look.

例句 ■■ The building **looks spick and span** after the renovation.

出處 ■■ 丘崇 · 重修羅池廟記："煥然一新，觀者嗟異。"

反義：原封不動	To be left intact.

shà fèi kǔ xīn
煞費苦心
Rack one's brains.

Make every effort.
Take great pains.
With much ado.

例句 ■■ We **racked our brains** to find a way to escape.

反義：漠不關心　Not to care a hang.

dāng jī lì duàn
當機立斷
Fish or cut bait.

Take the bull by the horns.
To think on one's feet.
Quick to act.

例句　Take action at this critical moment should be a to **fish or cut bait** decision.

出處　文選・陳琳・答東阿王箋：「拂鐘無聲，應機立斷。」

同義：快刀斬亂麻　Cut the Gordian knot.

反義：猶疑不決　To shilly-shally.

十三畫

wàn gǔ cháng qīng
萬古常青
Ever new.

Their names liveth for evermore.
Keep someone's memory green.

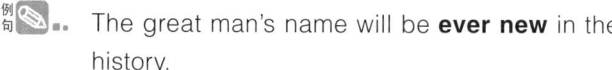

例句 📝 ▪ The great man's name will be **ever new** in the history.

> **同義：** 永垂不朽　Go down to posperity.

wàn zhòng yì xīn

萬眾一心

United as one.

Of one mind.

例句 📝 ▪ All parties are **united as one** to oppose the proposal.

出處 📝 ▪ 後漢書 · 朱儁傳："萬人一心，猶不可當，況十萬乎。"

> **同義：** 眾志成城　Unity is strength.

> **反義：** 各有打算
> The donkey means one thing, and the driver another.

zhì zhī nǎo hòu

置之腦後

Banish from thought.

Consign to oblivion.
Put out of one's head.
Think no more of (it).

 He had **banished** that event **from thought** years ago.

反義：仔細思量　Consult one's pillow.

zhì ruò wǎng wén

置若罔聞

Turn a deaf ear to

 The people have largely **turned a deaf ear to** the government's request for energy conservation.

同義：充耳不聞
None so deaf as those who won't hear.

反義：言猶在耳　Still ring in one's ears.

十三畫

yì bù róng cí

義不容辭

To be incumbent upon one.

Make a virtue of necessity.
Under a moral obligation.

 It **is incumbent upon you** to held these poor
people.

 三國演義："使玄德同力拒曹，……玄德既為東吳之
婿，亦義不容辭。"

同義：責無旁貸　To be duty-bound.

反義：多一事不如少一事　Leave well alone.

yì wú fǎn gù

義無反顧

With colours nailed to the mast.

Burn one's bridges.
Neck or nothing.
Go all lengths.
Go to a thing bald-headed.
To the bitter end.
Heedless of consequences.

例
句 ■. The people, **with colours nailed to the mast**, keep on to fight the invaders.

出
處 ■. 司馬相如・喻巴蜀檄：「義不反顧，計不旋踵。」

同義：捨得一身剮　To tempt providence.

---

qún cè qún lì
羣策羣力
Join forces.

Pool issues.

Put our heads together.

例
句 ■. All parties **joined forces** to fight for the ban of smoking in public places.

出
處 ■. 楊雄・法言・重黎：「漢屈羣策，羣策屈羣力。」

同義：戮力同心　To hang together.

反義：各有打算
The donkey means one thing, and the driver another.

十
三
畫

sì wú jì dàn

肆無忌憚

In defiance of the law.

To scruple at nothing.

例句 ▪. Actions **in defiance of the law** will get you nowhere.

出處 ▪. 禮記: "小人而無忌。"

同義: 為所欲為　To have one's own way.

反義: 投鼠忌器
Burn not your house to rid the mouse.

---

yāo chán wàn guàn

腰纏萬貫

Roll in wealth.

例句 ▪. He is **rolling in wealth** after he opened that restaurant.

出處 ▪. 明・陶宗儀・説郛・商芸小説: "腰纏十萬貫,騎鶴上揚州。"

同義：家財萬貫　Have money to burn.	
反義：囊空如洗　Dead broke.	

jiǎo tà shí dì
腳踏實地
Come down to bedrock.

Get down to brass tacks.
To be on firm ground.

例句 　One must **come down to bedrock** in dealing with people.

出處 　宋史・劉甲傳："甲嘗謂吾無他長，惟腳踏實地。"

同義：務實　Come down to earth.
反義：好高騖遠 　　　Gaze at the moon and fall into the gutter.

luò jǐng xià shí
落井下石
Take a mean advantage.

When a dog is drowning, everyone offers him a drink.

十三畫

例句 ■ The corrupted official **took a mean advantage** of that poor man by taking away his belongings.

出處 ■ 韓愈・柳宗元墓誌銘："落陷阱,不一引手救,反擠之,又下石焉者,皆是也。"

> **反義**:不為已甚
> Pour not water on a drowned mouse.

---

zhuāng mó zuò yàng
裝模作樣
To strike an attitude.

To be in borrowed plumes.
To make believe.

例句 ■ The man **stroke an attitude** and acted as if he is the boss.

> **反義**:拆穿西洋鏡　Take the mickey out of it.

---

zhuāng lóng zuò yǎ
裝聾作啞
Masters should be sometimes blind and sometimes deaf.

Feign ignorance.

例
句 ■■ Do not be trivial, **masters should be sometimes blind and sometimes deaf**.

出
處 ■■ 元曲選 · 馬致遠 · 青衫淚：" 可怎生裝聾作啞。"

> **同義：**隻眼開，隻眼閉　Wink at small faults.

guǐ jì duō duān
詭計多端
As crooked as a corkscrew.

Full of guile (tricks).
As crooked as a dog's hind leg.
As tricky as a monkey.

例
句 ■■ Do not trust Robert who is **as crooked as a corkscrew**.

> **同義：**老奸巨滑　As cunning as a fox.

> **反義：**誠實可靠　Fair and square.

dào mào àn rán
道貌岸然

Look as if butter would not melt in one's mouth.

例句 ■ The girl **looks as if butter would not melt in her mouth** when she sits next to her teacher.

出處 ■ 續仙傳： "李玨情景恬澹，道貌秀異。"

> **同義**：一本正經　　Have a serious look.

> **反義**：賊眉賊眼
> Have the brand of a villian in one's looks.

dào tīng tú shuō
道聽途說

Hear something over (through) the grapevine.

A traveller's tale.

例句 ■ I **hear over the grapevine** that you are moving to Shanghai.

出處 ■ 論語 · 陽貨： "道聽而途說，德之棄也。"

同義：街談巷議　Way-side inn gossips.

反義：權威人士透露
　　　　Straight from the horse's mouth.

guò mù bú wàng
過目不忘
Have a memory like an elephant.

A photographic memory.

例句 ✎ ▪ The boy **has a memory like an elephant**, he can tell you what happened in that period.

出處 ✐ ▪ 晉書・符融傳："符融下筆成章，耳聞則誦，過目不忘。"

反義：特別健忘　Have a head like a sieve.

guò yǎn yān yún
過眼煙雲
A flash in the pan

Ephemeral grandeur.

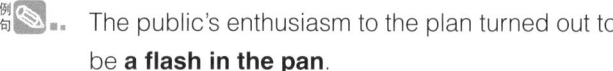

例句 ■■ The public's enthusiasm to the plan turned out to be **a flash in the pan**.

出處 ■■ 蘇軾・寶繪堂記："譬之煙雲之過眼，百鳥之感耳。"

> **同義**：曇花一現　Sudden glory soon goes out.

guò yóu bù jí
過猶不及

Overdone is worse than underdone.

The archer who overshoots misses as well as he that falls short.

In excess nectar poisons.

He that makes a thing too fine breaks it.

例句 ■■ You must not push your way too hard in the world as **overdone is worse than underdone**.

出處 ■■ 論語・先進："過猶不及。"

> **同義**：失之過甚　Carry too far.

> **反義**：聊勝於無　A little is better than none.

bǎo jīng fēng shuāng

飽經風霜

Gone through thick and thin.

Gone through deep waters.

例句 ✎ .. George has **gone through thick and thin** to become
an experienced expert in his trade.

同義：曾經滄海　To have sailed the seven seas.
反義：初見世面　Babes in the woods.

sēng duō zhōu shǎo

僧多粥少

Not enough to go round.

There are always more round pegs than square holes.

例句 ✎ .. Good jobs are **not enough to go round** for university graduates.

同義：杯水車薪　A drop in the bucket.
反義：綽綽有餘　Enough and to spare.

十四畫

shòu bǐ nán shān
壽比南山
As old as the hills.

Have a good innings.
Many happy returns of the day.

例句 The woman lived **as old as the hill** to become the oldest person in the world.

出處 南史・齊豫章王嶷傳："嶷謂上曰，古來言願陛下壽比南山，或稱萬歲。"

同義：壽同彭祖　As old as Methuselah.

---

mèng mèi yǐ qiú
夢寐以求
Hanker after

Long yearn for

例句 When I was a boy, I always **hanker after** being a writer.

同義：望眼欲穿　All agog.

duì zhèng xià yào

對症下藥

There is a salve for every sore.

Find a right antidote.

Counter with proper measures.

 We believe that **there is a salve for every sore** and the man's disease is curable.

> 反義：飲鴆止渴
>
> The remedy is worse than the disease.

kāng kǎi jiě náng

慷慨解囊

Loose the purse strings.

Come down handsome.

Put one's hand in one's pocket.

十
四
畫

 My friends **loosen the purse strings** to help people suffered from Tsunami.

> 同義：仗義疏財　Be a good Samaritan.

> 反義：吝嗇小氣　Cramp in the hand.

màn tiáo sī lǐ

慢條斯理
At a snail's pace.

As slow as molasses in winter.
Make two bites of a cherry.

例句 The relief work was carried out in **a snail's pace**.

出處 儒林外史："怎的慢條斯理。"

同義：從容不迫　Take one's time.
反義：急如星火　In hot haste.

qí kāi dé shèng

旗開得勝
To start with a bang.

Get off to a flying start.
At one stroke.
Get off the ground.

例句 Our school football team **started with a bang** in the match yesterday with a score of four to one.

同義：開門紅　The first blow is half the battle.
反義：出師不利　Step off on the wrong foot.

qí gǔ xiāng dāng

旗鼓相當

A drawn game.

A Roland for and Oliver.
To be well-matched.
A ding-dong fight.
On a par with
Six of one and half a dozen of the other.

例句 Both teams are of the same strength and played **a drawn game** yesterday.

出處 三國志・管輅傳注：「單子春日，吾欲自與卿旗鼓相當。」

同義：勢均力敵　Evenly matched.
反義：相形見絀　Cast into the shade.

十
四
畫

chàng suǒ yù yán

暢所欲言

Speak one's mind.

Open one's budget.

例句 I haven't seen George for years, so I **speak my mind** with him at the coffee shop.

同義：傾吐衷情　Get it off one's chest.
反義：半吞半吐　To mince matters.

dī shuǐ chuān shí

滴水穿石

Constant dripping wears away the stone.

Feather by feather the goose is plucked.
Slow but sure wins the race.
A sheer strength of will.

 Be determined to stick it out as **constant dripping wears away the stone**.

同義：持之以恆　Perseverance will prevail.
反義：三天打魚，兩天曬網　By fits and starts.

mò bù guān xīn

漠不關心

Not care a bit.

To fiddle while Rome is burning.
Not to care a hang (damn).

Devil-may-care.

 The miser does **not care a bit** about the sufferings of the people in the devasted area.

 韓愈：〝漠然不加喜戚於其心。〞

同義：毫不在意　Not to give a damn.

| 反義：多方照顧　Heap favours upon. |

mǎn fù jīng lún

滿腹經綸

Well versed in

Give chapter and verse.
A walking dictionary.
Widely read.

 The scholar is **well versed in** Chinese classics.

同義：博學多才　Know a thing or two.

| 反義：一竅不通　All Greek to one. |

十四畫

màn bù jīng xīn

漫不經心

Totally unconcerned.

Devil-may-care.
Pay no heed to

 The drunkard is **totally unconcerned** about his own health.

同義：毫不在意　To make nothing of
反義：全神貫注　Focus one's attention on

xī xī rǎng rǎng

熙熙攘攘

Hustle and bustle.

Bustling with activity.

 There is much **hustle and bustle** in the downtown area.

 史記 · 貨殖列傳： "天下熙熙，皆為利來，天下攘攘，皆為利往。"

同義：絡繹不絕　An endless flow.

jìn shàn jìn měi

盡善盡美

The pink of perfection.

Leaving nothing to be desired.
Tip-top.

例句 ■ She is **the pink of perfection** in the theaterical circle.

出處 ■ 論語：〝子謂韶，盡美矣，又盡善也。〞

> **同義：**十全十美　All as it should be.

> **反義：**腐敗透頂　Rotten to the core.

huò bù dān xíng

禍不單行

It never rains but it pours.

Misfortunes seldom come singly.
One misfortune comes on the neck of another.
Troubles never come singly.

例句 ■ Ben had lost his boy before he suffered from his bankrupt – **it never rains but it pours**.

出處 ■ 傳燈錄·紫桐和尚：〝禍不單行，福無雙至。〞

> **同義**：一波未平，一波又起
> Hit one snag after another.

> **反義**：福無雙至　Opportunity seldom knocks twice.

huò cóng kǒu chū
禍從口出

The tongue talks at the head's cost.

例句 ■■ Silence is good as **the tongue talks at the head's cost**.

出處 ■■ 傅玄・口銘：「病從口入，禍從口出。」

> **反義**：病從口入
> Gluttony kills more than the sword.

zhòng guā dé guā zhòng dòu dé dòu
種瓜得瓜，種豆得豆

As a man sows, so he shall reap.

If thou would reap money, sow money.

例句 ■■ George studied hard, so he got the scholarship–
as a man sows, so he shall reap.

出處 涅槃經："種瓜得瓜，種李得李。"

同義：前因後果　Cause and effect.

chēng xiōng dào dì
稱兄道弟
Call cousins with

Chum in with
Thick as thieves.

例句 Most Americans **call consins with** Canadians.

同義：拉關係　Cotton up to

反義：倒戈相向　Turn one's coat.

十四畫

jīng dǎ xì suàn
精打細算
Spare well and spend well.

Keep no more cats than will catch mice.
Take care of the pence and the pounds will take care
　of themselves.
Look at both sides of a penny.

Make every cent count.

On a shoestring.

 If you want to save money, you have to **spare well and spend well** with your poor salary.

> **同義**：該花就花，該省就省
> Spend not when you may save; spare not when you may spend.

> **反義**：鋪張浪費　Butter one's bread on both sides.

jīng míng qiáng gàn

精明強幹

To be up to snuff.

There are no flies on him.

To be on the ball.

 He **is up to snuff** in doing almost anything.

> **同義**：機靈果斷　Have the presence of mind.

> **反義**：低能差勁　Not worth one's salt.

jīng pí lì jié

精疲力竭

To be dead beat.

To be fagged (played) out.
Worn to a frazzle.
To be knocked up.
Ready to drop.

 Robert **is deadly beaten** because he worked late last night.

同義：百舍重繭　More dead than alive.
反義：神采奕奕　Full of pep.

jīng shén dǒu sǒu

精神抖擻

Keep one's pecker up.

Get one's tail up.
Bestir oneself.

 He always **keeps his pecker up**; nothing can discourage him.

 元曲選‧單鞭奪槊："你道是精神抖擻，又道是機謀通透。"

十
四
畫

同義：振作起來　To brace up.	
反義：委靡不振　In low spirits.	

chuò　chuò　yǒu　yú

綽綽有餘

Enough and to spare.

One's cup runs over.
Lashings and lavings.

例句 ▪▪ Don't worry about daily expenses, we have **enough and to spare**.

出處 ▪▪ 詩經 · 小雅 · 角弓："綽綽有裕。"

反義：借債度日　Live on ticket.

wéi　miào　wéi　xiào

維妙維肖

In bold relief.

True to life.
The very image of

The child is **in bold relief** with his father-like father, like son.

同義：栩栩如生	A speaking likeness.
反義：非驢非馬	Neither fish nor fowl.

yǔ zhòng bù tóng
與眾不同
To be a class by itself.

Out of the common run.
Out of the ordinary.

 That novel **is a class by itself** as it is written by an unknown writer.

同義：別開生面	Break fresh ground.
反義：平平庸庸	Pass in a crowd in a push.

zhēng zhēng rì shàng
蒸蒸日上
Grow with each passing day.

On the up and up.

Show increasing prosperity.

 The business **grows with each passing day**.

同義：欣欣向榮　Flourish like the green bay-tree.
反義：一落千丈　To go to pot.

guǒ zú bù qián
裹足不前
Hang back.

Fight shy of
At a standstill.
Drag one's heels.

 The shy girl **hung back** and refused to participate in the contest.

 李斯・諫逐客書："使天下之士，退而不敢西向，裹足不入秦。"

同義：停滯不前　Get bogged down.
反義：爭先恐後　The devil take the hindmost.

wù rù qí tú
誤入歧途
To have gone astray.

Drift off course.
Get lost.

 The boy **has gone astray** with bad friends and becomes the black sheep in our school.

> **同義：**迷失方向　Lose one's bearings.

shuō yī bú èr
説一不二
Mean business.

Mean what one says.
A bargain is a bargain.
A man of his word.

 When I give you my words, I do **mean business**.

> **同義：**説話算數　Keep one's word.

> **反義：**反覆無常　Blow hot and cold.

十四畫

bīn zhì rú guī
賓至如歸
Keep open house.

A home from home.
Feel at home.

 The lady is very kind and **keeps open house** to all new immigrants.

左傳 · 襄三十一年：“賓至如歸，無寧災患。”

qīng ér yì jǔ
輕而易舉
As easy as pie (pot).

Mere child's play.
Can do it on one's head.
Do something standing on one's head.
Duck soup.
As easy as anything.

 The job is **as easy as a pie** for George.

 詩經 · 大雅 · 烝民 · 朱熹注：“言人皆言德甚輕而易舉，然人莫能舉也。”

同義：不費吹灰之力　There's nothing to it.

反義：任務艱巨　A herculean task.

qīng miáo dàn xiě
輕描淡寫
To skate over.

Touch on lightly.

 He just **skates over** the fact.

同義：唱低調　Play something down.

反義：加鹽加醋　Tell with unction.

qīng jǔ wàng dòng
輕舉妄動
Act on impulse.

To rush headlong.
A leap in the dark.
Neck and heels.

 It is an important task which you should not **act on impulse**.

十
四
畫

韓非子・解老:"眾人之輕棄道理而易忘(妄)舉動者,不知其禍福之深大而道闊遠若是也。"

> **同義:**冒失從事　Buy a pig in a poke.

> **反義:**如臨深淵,如履薄冰　Tread as on eggs.

yuǎn shuǐ bú jiù jìn huǒ
遠水不救近火
Almost too late to do anything.

Water afar off quencheth not fire.

 I know you want to help, but it is **almost too late to do anything**.

 韓非子・説林上:"失火而取水於海,海水雖多,火必不滅矣,遠水不救近火也。"

> **反義:**近水樓台先得月
> The parson always christens his own child first.

yáo yáo wú qī

遙遙無期

One of these days in none of these days.

What may be done at any time will be done at no
time.
Till the cows come home.

例句　He said that the job will be done one of these days;
but **one of these is none of these days**.

> **反義：**指日可待　Before long.

sháo huá yǐ shì

韶華已逝

Have had one's day.

The mill cannot grind with the water that is past.

例句　Every dog at last will **have his day**.

> **同義：**光陰一去不復返　Lost time is never found.

> **反義：**年方弱冠　Arrive at majority.

十
四
畫

qí xīn xié lì
齊心協力
With united effort.

To join forces.

 With united effort of all nations, world peace can be maintained.

同義：羣策羣力　Pool issues
反義：各人自掃門前雪 　　　Sweep before your own door.

xū hán wèn nuǎn
嘘寒問暖
With kindest regards to

Present one's compliments to
Inquire after someone's health.
Give one's best regards to
Show every concern.

 I know the brothers well. So whenever I write letter to one of them, I always add one sentence: **With kindest regard to** your brother.

jiāo shēng guàn yǎng

嬌生慣養

Nursed in cotton.

Born with a silver spoon in one's mouth.

 That boy was **nursed in cotton**, easy to catch cold in winter.

同義：養尊處優　Lie on a bed of roses.
反義：牛馬生活　Lead a dog's life.

kuān dà wéi huái

寬大為懷

Do the handsome towards one.

To be large-minded.

 George **did the handsome towards the poor man**, giving him one thousand dollars.

同義：將相頭上堪走馬，公侯肚裏好撐船 　　　　Great gifts are from great men.
反義：心胸狹隘　A little pot is soon hot.

十五畫

yōu xīn chōng chōng
憂心忡忡
Afflicted with worry.

To have kittens.
To be on the rack.

例句 ■ She was much **afflicted with worry** at the bad news.

出處 ■ 詩經・召南・草蟲："未見君子，憂心忡忡。"

同義：惶惶不可終日　To be kept in suspense.

反義：無憂無慮　Happy-go-lucky.

lù lì tóng xīn
戮力同心
To hang together.

Unite as one.

例句 ■ Let's **hang together** to win the champion cup in the basketball game.

出處 ■ 墨子，尚賢："聿求元聖，與之戮力同心，以治天下。"

同義：同心協力	To pull together.
反義：各行其是	Have one's own way.

mó quán cā zhǎng
摩拳擦掌
Poised to fight.

Roll up one's sleeves.
Eager for the fray.
To square off.

例句 ■ All members of our school team are **poised to fight** and to win the game.

出處 ■ 元曲選　爭報恩："那妮子舞旋旋摩拳擦掌，叫吖吖
拽巷囉街。"

同義：躍躍欲試	Itch to have a go.

十五畫

fū yǎn sè zé
敷衍塞責
Huddle over one's duty.

To muddle through

例句 You **huddle over your duty** by your yes or no but no explanation to my question.

> **反義**：勉奮從事
> Keep one's nose down to the grindstone.

bào tiào rú léi
暴跳如雷
Fly into a passion.

To go berserk.
Hit the ceiling.
Get one's monkey up.
In a towering rage.
Stamp with fury.
Have a tantrum.
Blow one's top (stack).

例句 On learning the fact, Robert **flew into a passion** and slapped his desk.

> **同義**：怒不可遏　To hit the roof.

> **反義**：平心靜氣　Collect oneself.

mó léng liǎng kě

模棱兩可

Double talk.

Betwixt and between.
Answer like a Scot.
Cut both ways.

 There should be no **double talk** in your presentation at the negotiation table.

 舊唐書‧蘇味道傳："處事莫明斷，但模棱以持兩端可矣。"

同義：兩面討好　Sit on the hedge.

反義：一邊倒
All on one side, like Bridgnorth election.

lè jí shēng bēi

樂極生悲

He that talks much of his happiness summons grief.

Pleasure has a sting in its tail.

 Never be too happy in life as **he that talks much about his happiness summons grief**.

十
五
畫

出處 史記："酒極則亂，樂極則悲。"

> **同義：**興盡悲來
> He who laughs on Friday will weep on Sunday.

> **反義：**苦盡甘來　Pain past is pleasure.

tàn wéi guān zhǐ
歎為觀止
Nothing can be better.

The pink of perfection.

例句 You can say **nothing can be better** where you see his design.

出處 左傳‧襄二十九年："觀止矣，若有他樂，吾不敢請已。"

> **同義：**登峰造極　Reach the limit.

kuì bù chéng jūn
潰不成軍
To be put to rout.

To be utterly routed.

A crushing defeat.

 Your football team **was put to rout** by our school team yesterday.

> **反義：**得勝凱旋　Come off with flying colours.

shú néng shēng qiǎo
熟能生巧
Experience counts.

Practice makes perfect.

 After working as a cook for three years he has become the manager of the restaurant as **experience counts**.

> **同義：**功多藝熟
> He that shoots oft shall at last hit the mark.

rè lèi yíng kuàng
熱淚盈眶
Tears well up in one's eyes.

With eyes brimming with tears.

Watching that tragedy on the screen, **tears well up in the girl's eyes**.

同義：淚如泉湧　Break into a passion of tears.
反義：笑容可掬　A face wreathed with smiles.

qióng shē jí yù
窮奢極欲
Live on the fat of the land.

Live at rack and manger.
Fast living.

 The rich people are **living on the fat of the land**.

出處 漢書・谷永傳："窮奢極欲，沉湎荒淫。"

同義：糜爛生活　The primrose path.
反義：淡泊明志　Lead a stoical life.

qióng tú mò lù
窮途沒路
On one's beam-ends.

At the end of one's rope.

To be put to the pin of the collar.

To be at bay.

例句 ▪▪ Robert was **on his beam-ends** when people came after him for the debts.

同義：山窮水盡　To be on the rocks.

反義：錦繡前程　Have the ball before one.

yuán mù qiú yú
緣木求魚
To fish in the air.

Wring water from a flint.

Milk the bull.

Seek a hare in a hen's nest.

例句 ▪▪ Ask for a loan from that miser is to **fish in the air**.

出處 ▪▪ 孟子‧梁惠王上：“猶緣木而求魚也。”

反義：十拿九穩　Feel cork sure.

十五畫

péng tóu gòu miàn
蓬頭垢面

Like a brick-broom in a fit.

Look as if one has been dragged through a hedge backwards.

例句 ■■ The beggar looks **like a brick-broom in a fit**.

出處 ■■ 魏書："君子整其衣冠，尊其瞻視，何必蓬頭垢面，然後為賢。"

反義：瀟灑出塵　Neat but not gaudy.

---

shì kě ér zhǐ
適可而止

Keep within proper limits.

Let (Leave) well alone.
Know where to stop.
More than enough is too much.
Stretch your arm no further than your sleeve will reach.
Stretch your legs according to your coverlet.

例句 ■■ You may drink, but **keep within proper limits**, one or two cups is all right.

出處 ■■ 論語 · 鄉黨 · 朱熹注："適可而止，毋貪心也。"

同義：有分有寸　Draw the line somewhere.	
反義：有過之而無不及　Do a thing to a fault.	

shì dé qí fǎn

適得其反

Just the other way round.

Run counter to
The boot is on the other leg.
Just the reverse.

 You told him to go south, but it turned out to be **just the other way around** that he went north

同義：恰恰相反　On the contrary.	
反義：不謀而合　See eye to eye.	

zhèng zhòng qí shì

鄭重其事

To mean business.

In sober earnest.
In all seriousness.

Make a point of doing a thing.

 George **meant business** when he made the offer to Robert.

同義：慎重將事　Score twice before you cut once.
反義：等閒視之　Take things lightly.

xiāo shēng nì jì

銷聲匿跡

Make oneself scarce.

Drop out of sight.

 The man **made himself scarce** after the scandal.

 宋‧孫光憲‧北夢瑣言："銷聲匿跡，惟恐人知。"

同義：湮沒無聞　Sink into oblivion.
反義：一鳴驚人　Make a noise in the world.

yǎng zūn chǔ yōu

養尊處優

Live high off the hog.

Lie on a bed of roses.

Live in clover.

In the lap of luxury.

Up to the high-water mark.

Live like a lord.

Live the life of Rily.

To be on velvet.

 Rich people **live high off the hog** with hands in their pockets.

同義：嬌生慣養　Nursed in cotton.	
反義：潦倒一生　Down and out.	

jià qīng jiù shú

駕輕就熟

An old hand at the game.

Know the ropes.

An old ox makes a straight furrow.

例句 ■ George did the job very well because he is **an old hand at the game** with this work.

出處 ■ 韓愈文：〝若駟馬，駕輕車，就熟路。〞

> **同義**：老馬識途　An old dog for a hard road.

yā què wú shēng
鴉雀無聲

You would have heard a pin drop.

As silent as the grave.
Silence reigns.
A dead silence.

例句 ■ Students were so silent that **you would have heard a pin drop** when the schoolmaster came into the classroom.

出處 ■ 蘇軾詩：〝天風吹雨入闌干，烏鵲無聲夜向闌。〞

> **同義**：萬籟俱寂　As silent as the dead.

> **反義**：震耳欲聾　Split the ears.

mò shǒu chéng guī

墨守成規

To move in a rut.

Stick in the mud.
Follow the beaten track.

 No reformation can be seen as the new cabinet is only **moving in a rut**.

同義：照章辦事　Sign on the dotted line.
反義：自出心裁　Take the initiative.

tǐng ér zǒu xiǎn

鋌而走險

Take chances.

Take a bear by the tooth.
Sail close to the wind.
Take a risk.
Run a risk.

Think before jump, never **take chances**.

左傳・文十七年："鋌而走險，急何能擇。"

反義：明哲保身　Be worldly wise and play safe.

十五畫

fèn bú gù shēn

奮不顧身

Neck or nothing.

At all hazards.
To go all lengths.
Take one's life in one's hands.
Move heaven and earth.

 Neck or nothing, the fireman goes into the house to save the girl.

 司馬遷・報任少卿書："常思奮不顧身,以殉國家之急。"

同義:捨得一身剮　To tempt providence.
反義:畏縮不前　Back out of.

zhàn zhàn jīng jīng

戰戰兢兢

Shake in one's shoes.

To be on thin ice.
On the jig.
In a blue funk.
Very gingerly.

例句 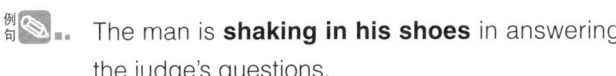 The man is **shaking in his shoes** in answering the judge's questions.

出處 詩經 · 小雅 · 小旻：「戰戰兢兢，如臨深淵，如履薄冰。」

> **同義**：臨深履薄　To tread upon eggs.

---

cāo zhī guò jí
操之過急
Jump the gun.

Draw one's bow before the arrow is fixed.
Leap over the hedge before one comes to the stile.

例句 Everyone in the line has his turn, you should not **jump the gun**.

> **同義**：欲速則不達　Haste trips over its own heels.

> **反義**：慢條斯理　Make two bites of a cherry.

---

cāo zòng zì rú
操縱自如
Like wax in one's hands.

As clay in the hands of the potter.

He is well experienced and handles the machine **like wax in his hands**.

> **反義：**老鼠拉龜，無處下手　To catch a Tartar.

tán huā yí xiàn
曇花一現
Sudden glory soon goes out.

A wonder lasts but nine days.
A flash in the pan.

 His reputation as a congressman was gone after the scandal as **sudden glory soon goes out**.

出處 妙法蓮華經 · 方便品第二："諸佛如來，時乃説之，如優曇缽花，時一現耳。"

> **同義：**過眼煙雲　Ephemeral grandeur.

héng chōng zhí zhuàng
橫衝直撞
Run amuck.

Run one's head against a post.
Jostle along.

Scared by the sharp sound, the donkey **ran amuck** at the market place.

> **反義：**躲躲閃閃　Sneaking in and out.

jī bù kě shī
機不可失
Take fortune at the tide.

One hour today is worth two tomorrow.

 That is a good offer and we should **take fortune at the tide**.

 舊唐書 · 李靖傳：「兵貴神速，機不可失。」

> **同義：**勿失時機　Now or never.

> **反義：**失之交臂　Miss the bus.

lì lì zài mù
歷歷在目
A commanding view.

A bird's eye view.
A full view.

十六畫

Fresh in one's mind.

例句 ■■ The fire is still **a commanding view** in everyone's mind.

出處 ■■ 杜甫・歷歷詩："歷歷開元事,分明在眼前。"

> **同義:**一目了然
>
> Everybody can see that at a glance.

rán méi zhī jí
燃眉之急
No time to be lost.

Pressing needs.
Not a moment to lose.

例句 ■■ **No time is to be lost** in the relief work.

出處 ■■ 五燈會元・蔣山法泉禪師:"問,如何是急切一句,師曰,火燒眉毛。"

> **同義:**火燒眉毛　Imminent danger.

> **反義:**不急之務　That can wait.

dú zhàn áo tóu

獨佔鰲頭

Come out first.

Sweep the board.
Carry off the palm.
Bear away the bell.

例句 ■■ George **came out first** in last year's contest.

出處 ■■ 洪北江詩話：〝俗語謂狀元獨佔鰲頭，非盡無稽。〞

同義：名列前茅　Head the list.
反義：名落孫山　Get plucked.

dú shàn qí shēn

獨善其身

Better be alone than in ill company.

Solitude is better than ill company.
Keep one's distance.
Keep oneself to oneself.

例句 ■■ When making friends, you better remember that it is **better alone than in ill company**.

出處 ■■ 孟子‧盡心上：〝窮則獨善其身，達則兼善天下。〞

十六畫

> **反義：**與世浮沉　To drift with the stream.

chēng mù jié shé
瞠目結舌
Struck dumb.

Stare tongue-tied.
Stunned and speechless.
To be dumb-founded.

 The accused was **struck dumb** by all those questions the judge asked.

> **同義：**目瞪口呆　Lose one's tongue.
>
> **反義：**鼓如簧之舌　Wag one's tongue.

jī shǎo chéng duō
積少成多
Many a mickle makes a muckle.

Every little helps.
Penny and penny laid up will be many.
Little and often fills the purse.

例句 ■■ We should spare less as **many a mickle makes a muckle** and so we may have enough for vacationing.

出處 ■■ 漢書·董仲舒傳：「聚少成多，積小致巨。」

> **同義**：集腋成裘
> Little by little the bird builds its nest.

> **反義**：坐食山空
> Always taking out of a meal tub, and never putting in, soon comes to the bottom.

 róng huì guàn tōng

融會貫通

Have at one's fingertips.

Know something inside out.
Have full comprehension.

例句 ■■ He **has at his fingertips** all about figures and that makes him a good accountant.

出處 ■■ 朱熹：「舉一而反三，聞一而知十，乃學者用功之深，窮理之熟，然後能融會貫通，以至於此。」

> **同義：**心領神會　To be on the beam.
>
> **反義：**一知半解
> Quarter flash and three parts foolish.

jǐn shàng tiān huā
錦上添花
Gild the lily.

Put the tin hat on.
To crown all.

 Do not **gild the lily** by contributing your money to a richman's club.

 王安石詩：「麗唱仍添錦上花。」

suí xīn suǒ yù
隨心所欲
At one's own sweet will.

Have it all one's own way.
At one's own discretion.
After one's own heart.
Do as one pleases.

Robert thinks that if he has money, he can do anything **at his own sweet will**.

同義：如願以償　To have one's will.
反義：事與願違　Fall short of one's expectation.

suí yù ér ān

隨遇而安

Take things as you find them.

Being on sea, sail; being on land, settle.
Take the world as it is.
Able to sleep on a clothes-line.
Take what comes and be contented.

 New job is rare, so you better **take things as you find them**.

 清 · 劉獻廷 · 廣陽雜記："隨寓而安，斯真隱矣。"

同義：既來之，則安之　Take things as they come.
反義：見異思遷 Grass is always greener on the other side of the hill.

十六畫

tóu tóu shì dào

頭頭是道

To make headway.

Have the ball at one's feet.
Have the ball before one.
To be in the groove.

例句 ■ The boy is **making headway** in his mathematics.

出處 ■ 續傳燈錄・慧力洞源禪師："方知頭頭皆是道。"

mò mò wú wén

默默無聞

To be nobody.

To be no burner of navigable river.

例句 ■ It is no good **to be nobody** in one's lifetime.

出處 ■ 法書要錄："書之為用，施於竹帛，千載不朽，猶愈沒沒而無聞。"

同義：湮沒無聞　Sink into oblivion.
反義：一鳴驚人　Make a noise in the world.

yōu róu guǎ duàn

優柔寡斷

To be shilly-shally.

To be neither off nor on.

He lost his good chance because he **is shilly-shally** in making decisions.

韓非子・亡征："緩心而無成，柔茹而寡斷。"

同義：躊躇不決　Like one o'clock half struck.

反義：快刀斬亂麻　Cut the Gordian knot.

yìng fù zì rú

應付自如

Equal to every situation.

Have a ready wit.
Take care of everything.

An experienced man is **equal to every situation**, dealing well with all people.

同義：縱橫捭闔　Wheel and deal.

yìng jiē bù xiá

應接不暇

Have one's hand full.

Have too many irons in the fire.
Up to one's ears in work.

 The manager **has hand's full** and he has to put your problem aside for the time being.

 世說新語 · 言語：" 從山陰道上行，山川相映發，使人應接不暇。"

> **同義：**分身乏術
> One can't be in two places at once.

liǎo rú zhǐ zhǎng

瞭如指掌

As plain as a pikestaff.

As plain as the nose in one's face.

 He knows the situation **as plain as a pikestaff**.

> **同義：**昭然若揭　All too clear.

> **反義：**如入五里霧中　To be lost in the cloud.

shēng míng láng jí

聲名狼藉

Earn oneself a bad name.

Fall into disgrace (discredit).

例句 ■■ The writer **earns herself a bad name** with her new novel on violence.

出處 ■■ 史記・蒙恬列傳：「惡聲狼藉，布於諸國。」

同義：名譽掃地　One's name is mud.
反義：名噪一時　To rise to fame.

dǎn xiǎo rú shǔ

膽小如鼠

As timid as a mouse.

Cannot say Boo to a goose.
Afraid of one's own shadow.
Have one's heart in a nutshell.
To be chicken-hearted.
As timid as a rabbit.

例句 ■■ She is **as timid as a mouse** and does not know how to answer the question.

> **同義：**前怕狼，後怕虎
> Too much taking heed is loss.
>
> **反義：**一身是膽　With plenty of guts.

kuài zhì rén kǒu

膾炙人口

Everyone speaks well of

To be in everyone's mouth.
Pass from mouth to mouth.
Enjoy great popularity.

 **Everyone speaks well of** the Chinese novel 'On The Watermargin'.

 唐音癸籤引埶圊擷餘："錢長信宜春句，於晴雪妙極形容，膾炙人口。"

> **同義：**家喻戶曉　To be a household word.

lín shēn lǚ báo

臨深履薄

Pick one's way (steps).

To tread upon eggs.

Keep on one's toes.

例句 ■■ He **picked his steps** when he started his business in this big city.

出處 ■■ 詩經‧小雅‧小旻：「戰戰兢兢，如臨深淵，如履薄冰。」

同義：戰戰兢兢　In a blue funk.

反義：莽莽撞撞　Like a bull in a china shop.

jǔ qí bú dìng
舉棋不定

Between hawk and buzzard.

Let "I dare not" wait upon "I would".

例句 ■■ Make your decission soon, to be **between hawk and buzzard** is to let your chance passing away.

出處 ■■ 左傳‧襄二十五年：「弈者舉棋不定，不勝其偶。」

同義：猶疑不決　Like one o'clock half struck.

反義：當機立斷　Take the bull by the horns.

táng bì dǎng chē

螳臂擋車

Kick against the pricks.

To bell the cat.

Throw straw against the wind.

 To complete with a giant establishment for market with your limited fund is to **kick against the pricks**.

 莊子‧人間世：〝汝不知夫螳螂乎，怒其臂以當車轍，不知其不勝任也。〞

同義：自不量力　Bite off more than one can chew.

---

qū yán fù shì

趨炎附勢

Hang on the skirts of

Hail the rising sun.

Come down on the right side of the fence.

 That guy **hangs on the skirts of** his boss to show how powerful he is.

 宋史‧李垂傳：〝焉能趨炎附勢，看人眉睫，以冀推挽乎。〞

十七畫

> **同義：**攀龍附鳳　Keep up with the Joneses.

zhǎn zhuǎn fǎn cè
輾轉反側
Toss about all night.

 He **tossed about all night** after the Tsunami news because he has many friends in that area.

 詩經‧關雎：＂悠哉悠哉，輾轉反側。＂

> **反義：**高枕而臥
> To be able to sleep on a clothes line.

bì zhòng jiù qīng
避重就輕
To ride off side issues.

It is better to fall from the window than from the roof. Of two evils choose the least.

 For such an important problem, you can't just **ride off with side issues**.

> **反義：**首當其衝　Bear the brunt of

qiè ér bù shě

鍥而不捨

Peg away at it.

Stick to it.
Firm and unyielding.

例句 To write a novel, one must keep **pegging away at it**.

出處 荀子 · 勸學："鍥而捨之，朽木不折，鍥而不捨，金石可鏤。"

同義：堅持到底　Go through with it.
反義：半途而廢　Do things by halves.

diǎn shí chéng jīn

點石成金

All he touches turns to gold.

A golden touch.

例句 He is such a clever businessman that **all he touches turns to gold**.

出處 列仙傳："許遜，南昌人。晉初為旌陽令，點石化金，以足逋賦。"

十八畫

反義：佛頭著糞　A fly in the ointment.

guī xīn sì jiàn
歸心似箭
Longing for home.

Christmas holidays will begin soon and all boarding students are **longing for home**.

同義：鳥倦飛而知還
Home is the sailor, home from sea.

反義：流連忘返　Can't tear oneself away.

guī gēn jié dì
歸根結蒂
In the long run.

In the final analysis.
When all is said and done.
As a result.

The market price will adapt to the real value **in the long run**.

zhān qián gù hòu
瞻前顧後
Take a look around.

Look about
Look round the corner.

 Take a look around when you make your plan.

出處 楚辭："瞻前顧後兮，相觀民之計極。"

> **反義：**肆無忌憚　To scruple at nothing.

lǐ shàng wǎng lái
禮尚往來
One good turn deserves another.

Give and take.
Kindness begets kindness.
Presents keep friendship warm.
He may freely receive courtesies that knows how to
　　requite them.
Ka me, ka thee.

 Do someone a good turn and he will do the same
　　to you as **one good turn deserves another**.

出處 .. 禮記・曲禮上："往而不來，非禮也，來而不往，亦
非禮也。"

同義：投桃報李　Exchange of gifts.

反義：雞犬之聲相聞，而老死不相往來
Half the world knows not how the other half
lives.

十八畫

---

fù shuǐ nán shōu
覆水難收
It is no use crying over spilt milk.

What is done can't be undone.

例句 .. What you have done is done and **it is no use to
cry over spilt milk**.

出處 .. 類林："太公曰，若能離更合，覆水定難收。"

---

jǐn yán shèn xíng
謹言慎行
Watch one's step.

Mind one's P's and Q's.
Say well, or be still.
Speak fitly, or be silent wisely.

You better **watch your steps** in dealing with your boss.

同義：小心戒慎　Take heed is a good rede.
反義：放蕩不羈　Have one's fling.

zhuǎn bài wéi shèng
轉敗為勝
Pull out of the fire.

Snatch a victory out of defeat.
Turn the tables on
Save the day.

 The team was **put out of the fire** in yesterday's match.

 史記："其為政也，善因禍而為福，轉敗而為功。"

zá luàn wú zhāng
雜亂無章
Higgledy-piggledy.

All in a muddle (mess).

例句 ▪▪ The room is in a **higgledy-piggledy** order.

出處 ▪▪ 韓愈‧送孟東野序：「其為言也，雜亂而無章。」

> **同義：**亂七八糟　At sixes and sevens.

> **反義：**有條不紊　In apple-pie order.

biān cháng mò jí
鞭長莫及

Beyond one's grasp.

Out of reach.

例句 ▪▪ I cannot help him because it is **beyond my grasp**.

出處 ▪▪ 左傳：「雖鞭之長，不及馬腹。」

> **同義：**遠水不救近火
> Water afar off quencheth not fire.

> **反義：**信手拈來　Come in handy.

qí hǔ nán xià
騎虎難下
On the horns of a dilemma.

He who rides on a tiger can never dismount.
Hold a wolf by the ears.
Needs must when the devil drives.
To be up a tree.
Up a gum-tree.

 Both designs are good, the judges are **on the horns of a dilemma** to decide which one is better.

 隋書 · 獨孤皇后傳："大事已然，騎虎之勢，必不得下。"

> **同義：**欲罷不能　To have a wolf by the ears.

lú shān zhēn miàn mù
廬山真面目
One's true self.

Come out in one's true colours.

 His deeds exposed **his true self**.

 蘇軾詩："不識廬山真面目，只緣身在此山中。"

反義：喬裝打扮　Sail under false colours.

wěn zhā wěn dǎ
穩紮穩打
Slow but sure wins the race.

Take no chances.
Play safe.
Play for safety.
Inch forward.

 Don't be hasty to take action, **slow but sure wins the race**.

同義：步步為營　Pick one's steps.

反義：速戰速決　Get it over and done with.

diān pèi liú lí
顛沛流離
Live a vagabond life.

Here today and gone tomorrow.
Have got the key of the street.

例句 ■. We all **lived a vagabond** life during wartime.

出處 ■. 論語："造次必如是，顛沛必如是。"

> **同義**：流浪漢　A bird of passage.

> **反義**：安家落戶　To settle down.

diān dǎo shì fēi
顛倒是非
Stand truth on its head.

Confound right with wrong.
Turn things upside down.

例句 ■. To say black is white is to **stand truth on its head**.

出處 ■. 韓愈・施先生墓銘："箋註紛羅，顛倒是非。"

> **反義**：撥亂反正　Set things right side up.

xuán ér wèi jué
懸而未決
Hang in the balance (wind).

Left in the air.
To be at stake.

The case is **hanging in the balance**, waiting for the final decission.

lú huǒ chún qīng

爐火純青

To have smelt the smell of fire.

Make oneself master of

 George **has smelt the smell of fire,** well experienced in dealing with such people.

二十畫

yào wǔ yáng wēi

耀武揚威

Bluff and bluster.

Brandish one's sword.
Swagger about.
Sabre-rattling.

 Soldiers of the victorious army **bluff and bluster** around the town.

 元曲選・無名氏・謝金吾三：「他也會斬將搴旗，耀武揚威，普天下哪一個不識的他是楊無敵。」

> **同義：**大張旗鼓　　With great fanfare.

chóu chú mǎn zhì
躊躇滿志

To one's heart's content.

To be self-satisfied.
Puffed up with pride.
Look like the cat that ate (swallowed) the canary.

例句 ■■ With your academic achievement, you may play **to your heart's content** during the vacation.

出處 ■■ 莊子：" 為之躊躇滿志。"

> **同義：**心滿意足　　After one's own heart.

> **反義：**大喊倒霉　　Get it in the neck.

yuè yuè yù shì
躍躍欲試

Loaded for bear.

As keen as mustard.
Have an itch to
Itch to have a go.

The worker, like a **loaded bear**, wants to start the machine at once.

成語故事：The proof of the pudding is in the eating

布丁是否味美，要吃了才可以證明，空談不如實據也。英國諷刺作家 Jonathan Swift（斯威夫特，1667-1745。Gulliver's Travels《格立弗遊記》有關於大人國和小人國的描寫。）主編的 A Complete Collection of Genteel and Ingenious Conversation（雅語妙句集）中有這樣的問答："Do you love pudding?" – "I love everything good; but the proof of the pudding is the eating." 好的東西人人喜歡，但是否真好還要試過才得到證實。

二十一畫

tiě shí xīn cháng
鐵石心腸
Hard-boiled.

Heart of marble.
To be hardhearted.
Dead to all feelings.
As hard as a stone (nails).

Even a **hard-boild** man could not be sad enough to see the tragic scene.

 皮日休賦序："余嘗慕宋廣平之為相，疑其鐵腸與石心，然睹其梅花賦，清便富艷，殊不類其為人。"

> **同義**：無動於衷　A heart insusceptible of pity.

tiě chǔ mó chéng zhēn
鐵杵磨成針
Little strokes fell great oaks.

Hair by hair you will pull out the horse's tail.
Perseverance will prevail.

 Be patient and determind, **little strokes fell great oaks**.

 源出李白少年時，遇老婦磨鐵杵作針，因發憤讀書。見《潛確類書》

> **同義**：水滴石穿
> 　　　Constant dropping wears away the stone.
>
> **反義**：一曝十寒　By fits and snatches.

hè lì jī qún

鶴立雞羣

A Triton among the minnows.

Stand head and shoulders above others.

例句 ▪▪ She looks like **a Triton among the minnows** among the girls.

出處 ▪▪ 世説新語：「嵇延祖卓卓如野鶴之在雞羣。」

> **同義：**出類拔萃　Tower above the rest.

quán yí zhī jì

權宜之計

Makeshift device.

Stop-gap measure.

例句 ▪▪ To delay any action is alway a good **makeshift device**.

出處 ▪▪ 後漢書：「計日用之權宜。」

> **同義：**權宜行事
> If you cannot have the best, make the best of what you have.

二十二畫

huān tiān xǐ dì
歡天喜地

Seem to tread on air.

 He **seems to tread on air** on learning that he has been accepted by that university.

 西廂記：　"則見他歡天喜地，謹依來命。"

同義：喜氣洋洋　Light up with pleasure.	

反義：愁眉苦臉　Wear a glum countenance.	

tìng tiān yóu mìng
聽天由命

Man proposes and God disposes.

Submit to Providence.
Resigned to one's fate.
Trust to chance.
Leave things to chance.
In the lap of the gods.

 Just do your best as **man proposes and God disposes**.

同義：坐以待斃　A close mouth catches no flies.

反義：人定勝天 Everyone is the maker of his own fate.

tīng qí zì rán
聽其自然
Let alone.

Live and let live.
Let things slide.
Give loose rein to something.

例句 ✎ **Let** the problem **alone** and it may be solved in time.

同義：放任自流　Let it run its course.

二十二畫

tīng qí yán ér guān qí xíng
聽其言而觀其行
Handsome is as handsome does.

Of him that speaks ill consider the life more than the word.

A statesman, as **handsome is a handsome does**, is judged by his words and deeds.

jiāo bīng bì bài
驕兵必敗
Pride will have a fall.

Pride goes before, and shame follows after.

 An arrogant person will fail in the long run as **pride will have a fall**.

 漢書："恃國家之大，矜人庶之眾，欲見威於敵者，謂之驕兵，兵驕者滅。"

biàn huàn mò cè
變幻莫測
The unexpected always happens.

 Be prepared for the worst as **the unexpected always happens**.

同義：天有不測之風雲
Though the sun shines, leave not your cloak at home.

反義：一成不變　Hard and fast.

jīng gōng zhī niǎo

驚弓之鳥

A burned child dreads the fire.

Once bitten, twice shy.

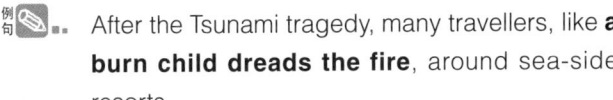 After the Tsunami tragedy, many travellers, like **a burn child dreads the fire**, around sea-side resorts.

出處 穀梁傳·成二年疏："敗軍之將不可以語勇，驚弦之鳥不可以應弓。"

同義：心有餘悸　He has seen a wolf.

反義：初生牛犢不畏虎
They that know nothing fear nothing.

jīng huáng shī cuò

驚惶失措

To be in a flat spin.

Stand aghast.
To be taken aback.
Frightened out of one's wits.
Shake in one's shoes.
Like ducks in a thunder-storm.

二十三畫

George **was in a flat spin** by the sudden visit of his boss.

同義：不知所措	At a loss what to do.
反義：不慌不忙	Keep one's head.

成語故事：Like father like son

　　一般譯作：有其父必有其子。此語中的 like 是形容詞，作"相似"解。因此它的意思是説父子不相爭，尤其是兒子和父親相似者。這是一句古諺，羅馬時代已經流行，十五世紀期間傳入英國。從前這句話還有一個尾句作：Like father like son; like mother like daughter。有其父必有其子，有其母必有其女。聖經舊約中有引用後半句者，見於以斯帖記中。人們常將"有其父必有其子"看作貶語，其實僅指相似。

yù bàng xiāng chí yú rén dé lì

鷸蚌相持，漁人得利

Two dogs fight for a bone, and a third runs away with it.

 George got elected while other candidates were quarrelling, **two dogs fight for a bone, and a third runs away with it**.

 戰國策：〝蚌方出曝而鷸啄其肉，蚌合而鉗其喙。兩者不肯相舍，漁者得而並禽之。〞

líng jī yí dòng

靈機一動

Take a notion.

Have a brain wave.
Take it into one's head.
Have a brilliant inspiration.
Hit upon an idea.

 Watching the movie, Robert **took a notion** from the hero's words and made up his mind.

反義：冥頑不靈　As stiff as a poker.

二十四畫

商務印書館 讀者回饋咭

　　請詳細填寫下列各項資料，傳真至 2565 1113，以便寄上本館門市優惠券，憑券前往商務印書館本港各大門市購書，可獲折扣優惠。

所購本館出版之書籍：＿＿＿＿＿＿＿＿＿＿＿＿＿＿＿＿＿＿＿＿＿＿

購書地點：＿＿＿＿＿＿＿＿＿＿＿＿＿　姓名：＿＿＿＿＿＿＿＿＿＿＿

通訊地址：＿＿＿＿＿＿＿＿＿＿＿＿＿＿＿＿＿＿＿＿＿＿＿＿＿＿＿＿

電話：＿＿＿＿＿＿＿＿＿＿＿＿＿　傳真：＿＿＿＿＿＿＿＿＿＿＿＿＿

電郵：＿＿＿＿＿＿＿＿＿＿＿＿＿＿＿＿＿＿＿＿＿＿＿＿＿＿＿＿＿＿

您是否想透過電郵或傳真收到商務新書資訊？　1□是　2□否

性別：1□男　2□女

出生年份：＿＿＿＿＿＿年

學歷：　1□小學或以下　2□中學　3□預科　4□大專　5□研究院

每月家庭總收入：1□HK$6,000以下　2□HK$6,000-9,999
　　　　　　　　3□HK$10,000-14,999　4□HK$15,000-24,999
　　　　　　　　5□HK$25,000-34,999　6□HK$35,000或以上

子女人數(只適用於有子女人士)　1□1-2個　2□3-4個　3□5個以上

子女年齡(可多於一個選擇)　1□12歲以下　2□12-17歲　3□18歲以上

職業：1□僱主　2□經理級　3□專業人士　4□白領　5□藍領　6□教師　7□學生
　　　8□主婦　9□其他

最常前往的書店：＿＿＿＿＿＿＿＿＿＿＿＿＿＿＿＿＿＿＿＿＿＿＿＿

每月往書店次數：1□1次或以下　2□2-4次　3□5-7次　4□8次或以上

每月購書量：1□1本或以下　2□2-4本　3□5-7本　4□8本或以上

每月購書消費：　1□HK$50以下　2□HK$50-199　3□HK$200-499　4□HK$500-999
　　　　　　　　5□HK$1,000或以上

您從哪裏得知本書：1□書店　2□報章或雜誌廣告　3□電台　4□電視　5□書評/書介
　　　6□親友介紹　7□商務文化網站　8□其他(請註明：＿＿＿＿＿＿＿＿＿)

您對本書內容的意見：＿＿＿＿＿＿＿＿＿＿＿＿＿＿＿＿＿＿＿＿＿＿
＿＿＿＿＿＿＿＿＿＿＿＿＿＿＿＿＿＿＿＿＿＿＿＿＿＿＿＿＿＿＿＿

您有否進行過網上購書？　1□有 2□否

您有否瀏覽過商務出版網(網址：http://www.commercialpress.com.hk)？1□有　2□否

您希望本公司能加強出版的書籍：1□辭書　2□外語書籍　3□文學/語言　4□歷史文化
　　　5□自然科學　6□社會科學　7□醫學衛生　8□財經書籍　9□管理書籍
　　　10□兒童書籍　11□流行書　12□其他(請註明：＿＿＿＿＿＿＿＿＿)

根據個人資料「私隱」條例，讀者有權查閱及更改其個人資料。讀者如須查閱或更改其個人資料，請來函本館，信封上請註明「讀者回饋咭-更改個人資料」

香港筲箕灣

耀興道 3 號

東滙廣場 8 樓

商務印書館 (香港) 有限公司

顧客服務部收